No Boundaries

NO BOUNDARIES

Prose Poems by 24 American Poets

Edited by

Ray Gonzalez

TUPELO PRESS

Dorset, Vermont

Cover painting *Crescendo* by Jean Morse

Cover and text designed by William Kuch, WK Graphic Design

CONTENTS

INTRODUCTION

In his 1916 Preface to *The Dice Cup,* French poet Max Jacob wrote, "I hardly know of any poet who's understood what it's all about and who's known how to sacrifice his ambitions as an author to the prose poem's formal constitution. Dimension counts for nothing in the beauty of a work, its situation and its style are everything. The prose poem must have, despite the rules which style it, a free and vital way of expressing itself." Almost one hundred years later, Jacob's statement holds true. Poets struggle constantly to get out of the way of their linear poems, even if the subject is their precious, personal world. The abundance of prose poems now being written reflects this endless struggle with ambition, but it also says more poets are bouncing off the transparent walls of paragraphs, their dimensional egos left somewhere in the branches of traditional, linear forms.

If Jacob is correct and the form depends on a specific style, it is also a constitution that explodes with something only prose poems give us. Each poem never ends and this is one kind of magnet that draws writers to prose poetry. Over time, some are "cured" of their linear accesses and never have to face a line break in their life again. The sacrifice of ambition? The beauty of a work? Jacob also wrote, "When one paints a picture, it changes completely with each touch, it turns like a cylinder and is almost endless." Ambition and beauty may actually be what the poet cannot sacrifice, thus the turning toward the prose poem as the complete literary act that defies the union between words and the self. What is the result of this defiance? Perhaps, it is the image and its visual text that do not give in to any kind of ending. There is a constant debate among practitioners of the prose poem over priorities—medium versus subject, the endless debate within any approach to poetry. The result may be the paragraph as poem and the poem as paragraph revolving around a vision that never separates the chosen language and sentence from their blossoming experience.

In the last half of the twentieth century, the prose poem has become one of the most dynamic styles of poetry worldwide. Poets who have established careers in lyrical, lined poetry are writing more prose poems. Younger, beginning poets are receiving critical acclaim and publication through prose poetry, with fewer of them depending on regular styles of verse to achieve success. As more poets write prose poems, one of the most common reason they give for turning to them is that their fluent composition offers a "freedom of expression" lined poetry often restricts. To many, this sounds like a contradiction stemming from the eternal belief that any kind of good poetry has no boundaries. Yet, those who write prose poems insist the act of placing their poems into sentences and paragraphs gives them a fresh approach to content and form.

Prose poetry encourages both experimentation and a resurgence of conventional modes of expression. Poets from various avant-garde movements often rely on prose poetry to break new ground. Writers who depend on imagistic, associative connections between personal experience and the traditional lyric find the prose poem reinforces fresh use of tone, metaphor, and syntax. Prose poetry is achieving a new level of creation and acceptance because it is the ideal mode for poets of different sensibilities and approaches. Perhaps, most important of all, is the fact prose poems have awakened the U.S. poetry world by leaving the worn out and expected framework of linear verse behind. Stanzas, line breaks, and white space on the page have been uprooted as prose poetry has chosen to condense form, while it has given poetic language new life. The prose poem shrinks what is visually seen on the page, but as the tension between lines and words build upon each other, what arises goes beyond traditional ideas of a uniform, sacred, and ordered space for poetry.

In his long out of print anthology. *The Prose Poem* (Laurel, 1976), poet Michael Benedikt defines a prose poem as "a genre of poetry, self-consciously written in prose, and characterized by the intense use of virtually all the devices of poetry, which includes the intense use of devices of verse. The sole exception to access to the possibilities, rather than the set priorities of verse is, the line break." Benedikt lists what he calls the "special properties" of the prose poem as its "attention to the unconscious, and to its particular logic; an accelerated use of colloquial and everyday speech patterns; a visionary thrust; a reliance on humor and wit; and an enlightened doubtfulness, or hopeful skepticism." He traces the development of the prose poem from the French Symbolists like Aloysius Bertrand and Charles Baudelaire to its growing presence in American poetry. These exact statements by Benedikt have been quoted in a number of essays on the genre because they come to the point about a writing that is frequently misunderstood because it does not easily lend itself to definition or interpretation, and does not need to use the literary road map many schools of modern poetry have followed to leave their mark in a highly competitive culture.

Twenty-five years after Benedikt's groundbreaking anthology was published, the prose poem is a major element in the vibrant and diverse poetry scene in the U.S., with its many practitioners acknowledging the foreign influence on their work. Peter Johnson, whose journal *The Prose Poem:* was a crucial venue for many important prose poets, may have said it best in his introduction to *The Best of the Prose Poem,* the anthology White Pine Press published to commemorate his years of hard work and devotion to the genre. Admitting it is hard to pin down the character of the prose poem, Johnson stated the form found life in the dual worlds of prose and poetry. That simple. Even more direct, he agreed with many of its writers that unpredictability remains one of its strongest aspects. For most styles and schools of poetry, whose leaders and imitators jockey for position to be deconstructed and blessed in critical texts, unpredictability is dismissed as too general a term. For the writers of prose poems, no specific tag or entry into the magic of constructing prose poetry is necessary. This is not the easy way out of critical analysis, or a call for a layman's paradise. It is an acknowledgment that the contemporary prose poem is a mature art form on its way to achieving the peak of its power and significance in American writing. No one out there is looking to impress any longer. The prose poem has found its place. The barriers set up by the poetry establishment against the success of the prose poem have been torn down with each succeeding decade and the handful of anthologies that have appeared since Benedikt's collection.

David Young, another poet, cites the lack of line structure in prose poems as an opening toward both "suggestiveness and completeness." These underlying and interactive tensions keep drawing more poets to its hypnotic possibilities. From early masters, like Bertrand, Baudelaire, and Max Jacob, to modern craftsmen Robert Biy, Russell Edson, and Charles Simic, the prose poem has always been on the leading edge of poetic development. Now, with an anthology like *No Boundaries* the circle becomes complete by gathering prose poets who have been writing long after the stage for what they do was set.

American literature was turned upside down in 1990 when Simic was awarded The Pulitzer Prize in Poetry for *The World Doesn't End* (Harcourt, 1989), his full-length collection of prose poems. Many critics and writers of traditional, "lined" poetry were in an uproar over this kind of recognition prose poetry received in the U.S. If the prose poem has emerged from a literary tradition going back two centuries, the opposition against it being recognized as a legitimate, vital aspect of contemporary writing is just as ancient. Yet, as American poetry today enjoys its largest audiences and more poets are writing and publishing, the place for prose poetry in this enormous community is being solidified. The linguistic power and unpredictability of its structure, and the fact a wide range of poets are writing it, makes the prose poem a magnetic guide toward the future direction of American literature.

No Boundaries reflects the present state of the prose poem in the U.S. It is does not encompass history nor does it try to be comprehensive. This book leaves the prose poem to itself, its creators, and its readers—perhaps the ideal environment for a rich and active genre. The poets in this anthology were chosen for five reasons: a) the quality of their work within the genre, b) their different styles and approaches to the prose poem, c) their influence on other poets, d) the fact many of these authors have published prose poetry extensively and have been some of the first whose work has helped to erase the boundaries between the linear and prose lyric, and e) my subjective tastes as the editor who has chosen a few individuals from a wide ranging and prosperous field of writers. By including ten poems by each poet, this book unveils the solid foundation of American prose poetry at the turn of the century. It calls for a close reading of each author's selections because their work, as a whole, is a key to experiencing and enjoying the restructured poetics of American writing. The extensive samples by each contributor show the depth and vision of poets devoted to the form.

Their commitment to a sustained vision allows the prose poem to live in today's complicated literary world, as each writer transcends the rich tradition that has made them a part of this kind of gathering. Theories on how the prose poem has evolved, and more detailed debates on where it belongs in the world of poetry, can be a part of a text that chooses the larger scope of historical tracings to achieve a grand picture of the art. *No Boundaries* says the prose poem has already been traced to this point in time and it is here, now, to be read and enjoyed. Its practitioners no longer need to wave the flag of poetic revolution because critics and canonical forces, that continue to search and document the long poetic road of American literature, have learned to leave the mysteries of the prose poem to the larger world.

NO
BOUNDARIES

NIN ANDREWS

Nin Andrews was born in Charlottesville, Virginia, and grew up on a farm, the youngest of six children. She studied at Hamilton College and Vermont College. She is the author of two books of prose poems, *The Book of Orgasms* (Cleveland State University Poetry Center, 2000) and *Why They Grow Wings* (Silverfish Review Press, 2001). Her chapbook, *Any Kind of Excuse,* won the Wick Chapbook Contest and will be published by Kent State University Press in 2003. Her translations of the French poet, Henri Michaux, appeared from Cleveland State University Press in 2002. The recipient of an Ohio Arts Council grant in 1998, her work has been published in many literary reviews and anthologies, including *Best American Poetry 1997* (Scribner), *The Best of the Prose Poem* (White Pine Press, 2000) and *The Paris Review.* She lives in Poland, Ohio with her husband and two children.

RED BLOSSOMS

The uncanny ability, an instinctual dance, a mind on safari, the scent of blossoms, the foraging flight, the uncanny ability, to cling, to find, to fly into a mind on safari, the scent of blossoms, feet as small as eyelashes, slipping in, an instinctual dance, a sign language, circling, slowly, crawling deeper, feet as small as eyelashes, into the tulip's center, a sign language, folding his wings, combing the surface with his tongue, crawling deeper into the tulip's center, spiraling down, folding his wings, combing the surface, the sugary juices, the warm petals, wind rustling leaves and ladies' dresses, spiraling down, pollen stuck to skin, hair, his wings, the sugars and juices of warm petals, rustling leaves and ladies' dresses, clutching the inner parts of the blossom, pollen stuck to legs, hair, wings, to the sweetness all over his fur, clutching the inner parts of the blossom, drunk with nectar, heavy, the sweetness all over his fur, the delirious silk of red blossoms, drunk with nectar, heavy, lifting up the delirious silk of red blossoms.

intentional
withholding of
an image as the
foundation for her
poem

THE ARTICHOKE

What an ugly specimen. The first time I saw it, I thought of Grandma's bathing cap, green and shrunken after all these years. I sliced it open, tasted the pale flesh, until gradually she offered herself up, leaf by leaf. In her depths she held a tiny, faded star, a spark that fell in a meteor shower over Frank's garden. Slowly I developed a taste for her expensive style: fancy restaurants, candlelit wines. Sometimes we stayed in and read by the fire, drinking the leftover melted butter, wiping the grease on our shirt sleeves. I introduced her to friends. Each of them adored her, said she was irresistible. She had the heart of a Buddha. Green leaves of flame. Nightly I grasped her like a seashell and listened to the nothing philosophers spend lifetimes writing about. Slowly she acquired the chilled look of a vegetable, kept in the icebox all day. Then one evening there were no leftovers. I went to the grocery store. The sales clerk said artichokes are out of season. This is not San Diego. Still I dreamt of her, dipped in lemony butter, scraped clean with the teeth and sucked, the pale cream of flesh, the tender flower, her skirt held up like a cup, each sip pulling me closer to the moon, the vegetable pearl of her insides where the heart fans out fibrous hairs and waits a last mouthful of her green world.

THE ULTIMATE ORGASM

For years I have been growing orgasms in a Petri dish. It's a costly and difficult task and would have been impossible without the expert help of renowned scholars whose lives have been devoted to the development and improvement of the orgasm. So far we have captured only a select number from the great variety available. When a volunteer comes into the laboratory, we do our best to describe the nature of our existing orgasms. We instruct and guide him or her on the proper courses of action, but it's impossible to know what you're giving a person. An orgasm can never be predicted. The orgasms come in many styles. Some are blanks. A few are silent and slip away without anyone knowing, making narrow escapes and blushing when you call their names. Others are scary. They use the body as a ventriloquist through which the stifled moans and tormented howls of cats and the murdered may be heard. Men think they'll die from the haunted orgasms. Women make no comment at all. But the best orgasms burst from a person like a cap off a Coke bottle and never come one at a time. These are the ultimate orgasms. When a person reaches the heights of the ultimate orgasms, we cannot contain our joy. We break open the champagne and cheer wildly.

THE OBSESSION

Occasionally the sailor has visions and sees a woman swimming nude beneath his ship, though, when he dives into the green waves, he finds only white jellyfish, opening and closing like small umbrellas. He remembers the time when he was a boy and imagined ordinary stones such as quartz and fools gold were valuable gems, lovely enough to win the heart of the girl next door. He never bothered to pick the stones up. Even then he knew the girl could never love him. The more he thought about her not liking him, the more he despised her and her adolescent beauty. The more he detested her, the more he wanted to watch her, follow her, sit behind her, and never let her out of his sight. That was the beginning of the obsession.

Evenings he stayed up late, peeking through his Venetian blinds, hoping to catch a glimpse of her in her pink striped pajamas. Every night of the week she would stretch out on the lime carpet in her living room and do her homework in front of the flickering TV. The boy began to believe that if he did not watch her, she might not do her homework. Then she might do poorly in school and be mocked, and he would have to protect her. What if he didn't know how? Better to be certain she did her work.

But the more he stared at her, the more beautiful she became, her skin softening, blushing, and sometimes the touch of her hair on his face wakened him from his dreams. He became convinced his eyes gave off a kind of glow that polished the girl, like an apple, that she could never have been as lovely if he had not looked at her so frequently, so intensely. He thought his staring might have made her breasts grow, just as the sun's heat and light can cause fruit to ripen.

That's when he realized her beauty was a kind of death wish. Like a mirage of an oasis in the Sahara, something that would enhance but never quench his thirst. No wonder years later he still saw her breasts in the middle of the sea. No wonder he hated her.

THE LIFE OF BORGES

The Borgesian sex life, the logic of minimal coitus and the womanless man is really quite simple. One lady fixed him for life. Once Borges slept with a prostitute, and the orgasm brought him so close to death, he feared it forever after. No one knows how she did it for sure. Perhaps she was an impenetrable mystery. A genuine ravaging sexual Pasiphae, an insatiable woman who lusted after white bulls. Maybe in the library of Babel, you can find her photo, writhing dangerously there between the pages and amidst descriptions of the various sources and of male unsexuality. In any case, Borges loved his mother too much. Everyone knows a man who loves his mother can never fully enjoy women.

The biographer of Borges dreamt of Borges, alive and warm, but not throbbing. He could not picture Borges, his own Borges, a man with unbridled imagination, loose on the body of a live woman. He knew that there was a reason, a terrible hidden secret.

Enter the prostitute. Of course, nobody saw her, and surely no one knew what Borges did with her. The reader of the biography of Borges does not need to follow the threads of his imagination into the locked room of Borges and the prostitute. Sparing us any unnecessary speculations, the biographer concludes: the orgasm almost destroyed our renowned Argentinean.

A Borges biographer understands such matters. He knows a man could be hurt for a lifetime after one night in bed with the wrong sort of woman. Of course, no one saw the biographer in bed with such a lady. Afterwards he might have told tales of a terrifying sexual episode, concluding with a volcanic climax, an eruption of dynamic proportions that shook the very center of his being while the woman lay calm and unmoved. Such occurrences could limit the future of even the healthiest young blade. I know. I shall restrain myself from exhaustive explanations. It is I alone who understands the biographer of Borges.

AN ALTERNATIVE TO SEX

In a desperate attempt to find an opening in my mind, the kind one travels in by submarine, I began to invent an alternative to sex. Something entirely new. Not that I was suffering a sudden attack of aphrodisia. Oh no. My feelings in all aspects of body and mind were quite alive. It occurred to me, of course, that one should not breathe too deeply, nor should one sigh. One absolutely must not pant because then the submarine windows would fog up, and I liked to imagine what I would see very clearly. Everywhere rushing, watery blue. Legs, of course, were folded neatly and clothed in sturdy pants, perhaps itchy woolen plaids. I kept my features calm, impassive. I arranged my face as one might a table setting or a bowl of fruit. I didn't shout or even whisper goodbye to sunlit sheets and pillows and the man who fit like favorite jeans.

No, I kept silent, snapped shut like a compact. I took pleasure in the cold flight downwards, and the feeling that I was falling down an elevator shaft. I couldn't help thinking that little deaths might be everything. I wondered what it might be like to drift in the open air, drying like laundry on a clothesline. If the door opened, would I be rushed to the sea tops? Would an extinct god from an unknown race lift me into the skies? Would I continue ascending like Mohammed's horse? Or would I capsize, plunge like a meteor, a ravaged, doomed sexual Napoleonette, with no alternatives but ecstatic regrets?

THE RIGHT TIME

Sometimes we are absolutely ready. Always at the wrong time, but sometimes it could be the right time. We look at each other, and we know. Time to take off our clothes. It is most inconvenient because precisely at that moment my grandmother arrives wearing a hat with ostrich feathers. And my Aunt Sheila who hates men, says all men will want me until I am fifty and molt. And my father who thinks pretty women are whores. And my mother who is eleven. They all arrive and tell me to cross my legs, keep my thighs pressed together. Sometimes Mr. Repolt arrives, too. He used to close his fingers around my naked knee like a cat's paw. They close in around us like a cat's paw, and there is nothing we can do about it but laugh nervously. Afterwards, we reason, if we were to remove our clothes, we would feel the world press its ears and eyes to our skin, and we would go cold. Even on the hottest days. We would apologize to them all for wrinkles and the odd mole or birth mark. We would wish we hadn't been seen like that. We know this because we never take off our clothes. We don't want to take the chance. We have everything to lose.

THE MESSAGE

She dreams of tracing the skin of this room: of you and the velvet hats with ostrich plumes and the china cups and the silver spoon that lightly rests inside, skimming the rim like a tongue.

Sometimes she surrounds you and breaks apart in tears or rain, you can't tell which, only the choking sorrow you feel and the loneliness. This is a message from the void that loves your many things, loves them so much it sobs.

LIKE AN ANGEL

The orgasm gradually disappeared from our lives. We imagined it had moved out to California and was now living in a distant city on ocean front property. We contemplated moving there ourselves, picturing the sunlit view from our glass house where tan men and women paraded about in swim suits and scanty lingerie, and orgasms occurred with the simplest acts such as the slipping on of silk gowns and sun hats or the combing of hair. We planned our future there among the orgasms. We stayed up in the dark, whispering long after the children were in bed, the soothing sounds of our hushed voices like the inane beating of insect bodies against the window on summer nights. But slowly we went silent. Now we pass by one another like somnambulists while sweeping floors and carrying baskets of laundry. The orgasms are lost inside us. We feel the wind of their wings as we brush against each other without even bothering to mutter excuse me. On the streets tires screech, and a light sweeps across our ceiling and walls and faces. For an instant I see your face illuminated. It looks like white stone in the sudden light. I see the orgasm like an angel inside that stone. I see you like a stone inside the angel.

AMNESIA

One summer I spent long hours with therapists. They were puzzled that I could never remember any details about my childhood, and when they fished into my unconscious, trying to loosen the buried memories of a girl, they found nothing but sunlight. One therapist interpreted it to be the light in an operating room. Or the light a person sees after being hit over the head with a brick, or when she dies and comes back to life. I was certain I had never been operated on, nor had I been bopped in the head. That's when I began to tell stories. I told them about angels I had seen turn into stone. I told them I had been adopted at age six by a hard-working couple who milked Jersey heifers for a living, that my first memories were of my tired parents and Madge, a red-haired woman who rented a stall in their cow barn where she boarded Jimbo, a dappled gelding. Madge dressed exclusively in lime green. Cashmere. Madge reminded me of lunar moths I sometimes saw on the naked light bulb at night. Once, when I skinned my knee on the gravel driveway, Madge dismounted Jimbo, picked me up, and hugged me close, pushing me against her huge lime-green bosoms. My lips and cheek brushed her face, and Madge felt smooth and slippery as soap. Nervously I bit into the soft skin around her fingers. When Madge bobbed away again on horseback, rhythmically lifting and lowering her buttocks, her sweatered breasts slow-dancing, I noticed how the eyes of the farm hands and my father slow-danced with them. Even then I knew that bosoms weren't just bosoms. Just as years later I would suspect that orgasms were not merely orgasms. They were tiny messages from the aliens, folded like cloth napkins in a linen drawer.

ROBERT BLY

Robert Bly is the author of numerous books of poetry, translations, and essays. Recent collections, all published by HarperCollins, include *The Night Abraham Called to the Stars* (2001), *Eating the Honey of Words: New and Selected Poems* (1999), *Morning Poems* (1997) and *What Have I Ever Lost By Dying?: Collected Prose Poems* (1992). New translations by Bly include *The Half-Finished Heaven: The Best Poems of Tomas Transtromer* (Graywolf Press, 2001) and *The Roads Have Come to an End Now: Selected and Last Poems of Rolf Jacobsen* (Copper Canyon Press, 2001), which was co-translated with Roger Greenwald and Robert Hedin. Bly's legendary literary journal, *The Sixties,* has recently appeared as *The Thousands.* Bly was awarded a 2002 Minnesota Book Award for Poetry for *The Night Abraham Called to the Stars.* He lives in Minneapolis, Minnesota.

WARNING TO THE READER

Sometimes farm granaries become especially beautiful when all the oats or wheat are gone, and wind has swept the rough floor clean. Standing inside, we see around us, coming in through the cracks between shrunken wall boards, bands or strips of sunlight. So in a poem about imprisonment, one sees a little light.

But how many birds have died trapped in these granaries. The bird, seeing the bands of light, flutters up the walls and falls back again and again. The way out is where the rats enter and leave; but the rat's hole is low to the floor. Writers, be careful then by showing the sunlight on the walls not to promise the anxious and panicky blackbirds a way out!

I say to the reader, beware. Readers who love poems of light may sit hunched in the corner with nothing in their gizzard for four days, light failing, the eyes glazed.... They may end as a mound of feathers and a skull on the open boardwood floor....

AN OYSTER SHELL

The shell is scarred, as if it were a rushing river bottom, scratched by the great trees being carried down. Sometimes its whitish calcium has been folded over itself, as when the molten rock flows out; so something is still angry.

When we turn it over, we feel that the shell on the inside is more secretive, more finished, more human. Our fingers feel the smooth inside and know of blueberries, earned pleasure, the sweet loneliness of the old man late at night, when angels keep looking for him in the early dawn, calling across the snow-covered fields.

THE CROW'S HEAD

Supper time. I leave my cabin and start toward the house. Something blowing among the tree trunks.... My frail impulses go to shelter behind thin trees, or sail with the wind. A day of solitude over...the time when after long hours alone, I sit with my children, and feel them near..... At what I want to do I fail fifty times a day, and am confused. At last I go to bed.

I wake before dawn hearing strong wind around the north bedroom windows. On the way to the cabin, I see dust of snow lying on yesterday's ice. All morning snow falls.

By noon I give up working, and lie listening to the wind that rises and falls. Sometimes it makes the sound of a woman's skirt pulled swiftly along the floor.... At other times it gives a slow growl without anger like the word *Enoch*....

I go to the window. The crow's head I found by the bridge this summer, and brought home, stands on the window sash. Feathers edge its Roman beak. It is fierce, decisive, the one black thing among all this white.

A HOLLOW TREE

I bend over an old hollow cottonwood stump, still standing, waist high, and look inside. Early spring. Its Siamese temple walls are all brown and ancient. The walls have been worked on by the intricate ones. Inside the hollow walls there is privacy and secrecy, dim light. And yet some creature has died here.

On the temple floor feathers, gray feathers, many of them with a fluted white tip. Many feathers. In the silence many feathers.

THE BLACK CRAB-DEMON

The ocean swirls up over the searock. It falls back, returns, and rushes over a whirlhole the shape of a galaxy. A black crab climbs up the searock sideways, like a demon listening in Aramaic.

All at once, I am not married; I have no parents; I wave my black claws and hurry over the rock. I hold fast to the bottom; no night-mother can pry me loose; I am alone inside myself; I love whatever is like me. I am glad no seabeast comes to eat me; I withdraw into the rock caverns and return; I hurry through the womb-systems at night.

Last night in my dream a man I did not know whispered in my ear that he was disappointed with me, and that I had lost his friendship…. How often have I awakened with a heavy chest, and yet my life does not change.

AN OCTOPUS

I hear a ticking on the Pacific stones. A white shape is moving in the furry air of the seacoast. The moon narrow, the sea quiet. He comes close; a long time the stick ticks on over the rock faces. Is it a postal employee saddened by the sleet? It comes nearer. I talk. The shape talks, it is a Japanese man carrying a spear and a heavy-bellied little bag. The spear has a hook on the end. What are you looking for, clams? No! Octopus!

Did you get any? I found three. He sits down. I get up and walk over. May I see them? He opens the plastic bag. I turn on the flashlight. Something wet, fantastic, womblike, horse intestine-like. May I take hold of one? His voice smiles. Why not? I reach in. Dry things stick to my hands, like burrs from burdocks, compelling, pleading, dry, poor, in debt. You boil them, then sauté them. I look and cannot find the eyes. He is a cook. He ate them in Japan.

So the octopus is gone now from the mussel-ridden shelf with the low roof, the pool where he waited under the thin moon, but the sea never came back, no one came home, the door never opened. Now he is taken away in the plastic bag, not understood, illiterate.

TWO SOUNDS WHEN WE SIT BY THE OCEAN

Waves rush up, pause, and drag pebbles back around stones...pebbles going out... It is a complicated sound, as of small sticks breaking, or kitchen sounds heard from another house.... Then the water draws down farther over the stones always wet.... Suddenly the sound of harsh death waves as the ocean water races up the roof of loose stones, leaving a tiny rattling in the throat as it goes out.... And the ecstatic brown sand stretched out between stones: the anger of some young women is right.

And always another sound, a heavy underground roaring in my ears from the surf farther out, as if the earth were reverberating under the feet of one dancer. It is a comforting sound, like the note of Paradise carried to the Egyptian sands, and I hear the driftwood far out singing, what has not yet come to the surface to float, years that are still down somewhere below the chest, the long trees that have floated all the way from the Pacific islands.... And the donkey the disciples will find standing beside the white wall...

CALM DAY AT DRAKE'S BAY

A sort of roll develops out of the bay, and lays itself all down this long beach.... The hiss of the water wall two inches high, coming in, steady as lions, or African grass fires. Two gulls with feet the color of a pumpkin walk together on the sand. A snipe settles down...three squawks...the gulls agree to chase it away. Then the wave goes out, the waters mingle so beautifully, it is the mingling after death, the silence, the sweep—so swift—over darkening sand. The airplane sweeps low over the African field at night, lost, no tin cans burning; the old woman stomps around her house on a cane, no lamp lit yet...

A PIECE OF LICHEN

This piece of dried lichen was clinging to a rockside in Maine, and I had to bend over, crouching on my knees, reach down over the side of the rock, to get it. It has the consistency of black Chilean deserts seen from the air.

The lichen piece looks like an ox-skin blown about in a dark Thor storm, flopping across the roads near Las Vegas, turning over and over, frightening rabbits and foxes as it rolls. Its edges turn up or under.

It's clear that something is falling out of this chalice now, as if its dried womb cannot contain what it once contained. Something is falling out as if the black one has made a move, as if the dry one will appear, has appeared, and we are in danger of being rolled over by black dryness—invisible in the dry black nights.

The lichen came away easily, was not deeply attached. When we turn it over, we know what it's like to have only enough water to carry you through half of the year.

When the thief who has stolen the blanket arrives back home, he throws the stolen blanket down in a corner of his room. If he folds the blanket, who is there to unfold it?

THE ORCHARD KEEPER

We walk together through the new snow. No one has walked through it or looked at it. The deep snow makes the sound the porgies hear near the ocean floor, the hum the racer hears the moment before his death, the sound that lifts the buoyant swimmer in the channel.

Four pigeon grass stalks, scarce and fine, lift their heads above the snow. They are four heron legs moving in white morning fog, the musical thoughts that rise as the pianist sits down at her table, the body laboring before dawn to understand its dream.

In our dream, we walk along a stone wall, and pause at an open gate. We look in at an orchard, where a fount of water is rising in the air. We see armed men lying asleep all around the fountain, each with his sword lying under him.
And the orchard keeper...where is he?

JOHN BRADLEY

John Bradley is the author of two full-length collections of poetry, *Love-In-Idleness: The Poetry of Roberto Zingarello* (Word Works, 1995) and *Terrestrial Music* (Curbstone Press, 2003). He is the editor of *Atomic Ghost: Poets Respond to the Nuclear Age* (Coffee House Press, 1996) and *Learning to Glow: A Nuclear Reader* (University of Arizona Press, 2002). His prose poems appear in the anthology *Best of the Prose Poem* (White Pine Press, 2001), the pamphlet *States of Common Rapture* (Red Pagoda Press, 2000), and the chapbook *Add Musk Here* (Pavement Saw Press, 2003). He teaches writing at Northern Illinois University in DeKalb.

HISTORY OF CLOUDS

The mold in the kitchen cupboard softly ticking. The three toes at the bottom of the potato sack. The chicken bone on the saucer huddling against the empty coffee cup. The sparrow with the small, egg-shaped songs in its chest. The principal who no one will tell has a slice of burnt toast on his right shoulder. The musician on the flight from Phoenix who knows, from the basil scent of the woman's hair in the seat ahead, he must compose a song for four saxophones and a kettle drum. The pilot who carries at all times a book, translated from the Chinese, entitled *The History Of Clouds.* The continents of water on the flat rooftop of the store that sells guns and tapes of the Elvis impersonator born in Iran. The pointed-toed shoe once used to stir a can of silver paint. The boy with a trombone case filled with the ducks he found along the shore of the reservoir. The first and the second and the third time the man in the Burger King orders French fries without remembering he just placed an order for French fries. The Greyhound bus traveling across Nebraska, each moment drawing nearer and nearer to Minneapolis without ever leaving Nebraska. The heavy luminescence around a missile underneath the prairie where a woman once played her flute for a lovesick buffalo. The snail shell fossil embedded in a shoulder bone unearthed by a road crew on Long Island. The whale who swallowed the hair of a violinist who lives in Tokyo and at that moment chokes on her glass of water. The AIDS patient who sees, each time he falls asleep, a hand wiping numbers off a white sign above the stack of green crates filled with clean glasses. The grinding of a root against the gas station's foundation. The mold in the kitchen cupboard softly ticking. My mother, in her long, turquoise bathrobe, wandering from room to room, trying to find the basement door.

PARABLE OF THE ASTRAL WHEEL

I wonder where your brother is, my father says, puffing on his briar pipe at the train station, gazing up at the portly pigeons in the rafters. The station has been closed for decades, but I don't tell him. *Should have been here hours ago,* he notes. I ask if I can polish his shoes. I open the wooden barrel that serves as my stool and storage unit, find the ox blood polish, open the can and spit into the polish as he taught me to do when I was a child. He pretends to read *Time* magazine, but I know he's studying my every move. When I'm done buffing his shoes to an obnoxious shine, I sit back and wait. He glances down at his shoes and says, *Just a little more spit.*

I ask him if he'd like a pack of gum, a comb, condoms, a radioactive tumbleweed, an astral prayer. I *wonder,* he says, what's keeping your brother. I don't tell him that my brother left us years ago. *He never would have left, you know, if I had read the Bible every day,* he tells me. *You'll like the astral prayer,* I tell him. *It's completely silent and no one can see it, and your every movement spins out a prayer.* He sadly shakes his head. *If only we had listened to the priest,* he says, *and when he was a baby had his little butt sewn shut.*

PARABLE OF THE TRAVELER FROM QATAR

When I returned from Qatar, I told Minnie and Jump and Willow and Tiger. I told Winnie and Lincoln and Roundel and Klank. Who told the grocer, who told the mail carrier, who told the FBI, who told me: *There is no such place as Qatar.*

I can truthfully tell you, my friends, that there was and, I believe, still is a Qatar, though I have only this faint recollection: A sleek city street with sleek, milky traffic and a large flashing sign that spoke in ninety-nine languages, telling all: *Behold Qatar.*

House arrest has led me to discover a new career—water colorist. Each day the Inspector brings me my groceries and art supplies. He leaves with my new shopping list and with that day's intelligence report—a water-color scene of Qatar.

No matter if I paint my mother in a sombrero in Phoenix, or an old Finn snoring on a bus in Duluth, or bowing gas station attendants in white uniforms and white gloves in Hiroshima. All witness that ever-so-distant place called Qatar.

HAWAIIAN SHIRT

Maybe I left it in the dressing room, the way I sometimes forget my ring on the ledge above the sink after washing my hands. How am I going to be able to relieve myself now? Shoulder me. At least I have my tongue. I know it was there when I was in the limo. I could feel the bulge in my pants as I watched the long legs of the yellow jacket delicately stroke the red pine needle on the windshield. Maybe it fell out of my pants when I left the dressing room. Shoulder me. At least I still have my retractable tongue. What would anyone want with a penis, anyway? A woman once told me she dreamed she was carrying my penis around with her all day long right there in her purse. I just smiled. This tv show said that after the slaughter at Sand Creek, soldiers rode off with the sexual skin of Indian women on their hats. Shoulder me. At least I still have my redoubtable tongue. If I wear the Hawaiian shirt with the red and purple pineapples, most likely no one will notice the void, shoulder me, shoulder me, in my pants.

UNFORGIVEN

Leaning over my bed, clad in a red thong panty and H_2O bra (with water-filled inner pockets creating the most natural addition to his bustline) was the one and only General Augusto Pinochet. Is he here to seduce me? To recite a Pablo Neruda love poem? To sell me C.I.A.-imported Viagra? To lead me in a prayer for Orlando Letelier, who died in a car bomb Letelier himself planted just to make Pinochet look bad? How quick I was to judge the General. All he wanted, he quickly explained while adjusting his water-enhanced breasts, was to borrow my flashlight, so he could find the toilet. He apologized, in his sincerest, nondictatorial, free-market tone, for disturbing me.

"But why the H_2O bra, General?" I inquired. "Not that I have anything against an organic, non-toxic approach to enhancing your bustline, of course."

"Cara, I've received such terrible press lately I thought I might be considered more, how do you say, more, more venereal..."

"Vulnerable?" I asked.

"Yes, yes, yes. Poor dispirited General Pinochet fannying about in lingerie. Do you think it will work? Should I have listened to those damned advisors with their Ph.D.s in Lingerie Studies?"

At this point he limped away down the hall. I could hear the homuncular grinding of spinal disk against spinal disk, as he muttered, "Oh, the paradoxical effects of Frederick's of Hollywood lingerie on the American public."

CRIMES AGAINST THE FUTURE

A man can't be held to blame for the stains on his sweat band, says a senator of the nominee to head the C.I.A. *If Jesus Christ wore a black bowler,* he tells the senate committee, *I believe his sweat band would be dark with sweat.* A gun goes off in the back of the post office. A filly in Cedar Lake is stabbed repeatedly. In Vincennes the Klan files a petition, a piece of ordinary paper with ordinary signatures, to march in the Vincennes homecoming parade. If Jesus Christ wore a black bowler. A man pays a woman 100 dollars to dance for him. An ordinary man, ordinary woman. In a G-string, she dances for him on the motel bed. Only for him. 200 times the filly is stabbed with a pitchfork. An ordinary pitchfork. Peroxide must be used to remove the blood from the horse's hide. Ordinary peroxide. The man pays 200 dollars to watch the woman masturbate. For him, only for him. *You have beautiful eyes,* the man tells her. *Bountiful skies,* the police in the adjacent room hear. They charge into the motel room, guns drawn. The man who shoots postal workers shoots himself. Brain dead, his organs are given away. Ordinary heart, ordinary liver, ordinary kidneys. *House of the Good Shepherd,* the Klan in Vincennes calls itself on its petition. A House where each inhabitant wears a black bowler. Nothing more. With a pitchfork handle the filly named Boo-Boo was beaten. An ordinary pitchfork handle. An ordinary filly. *You have beautiful thighs,* the woman in the G-string tells the policemen gathered around her. Each in a black bowler, the sweat bands dark with sweat.

TO PROPAGATE A CHANGE IN CONFIGURATION, OR BILL GATES
& THE BLUE COW

The cow had been shaved with a straight razor, perhaps a few hundred tiny purple nicks, and then painted Krishna blue. Bill Gates is a man. I am a bungalow man with a small white gate, therefore everything I own serves the only Bill Gates. The myth of the blue cow goes back to the invention of color tv. I was squatting in a split-level blue cow in Wayzata when I smoked for the first time blue cow dung. I willed my wastrel body along the railroad tracks over Lake Minnewawa, ready should the willing train appear amongst me to dangle by my fingertips from the trestle. If I had lived, I could have gone on to become another Bill Gates, says my mother. My little white gate does not open, so you must go around go around it. If Bill Gates was to compose a song, it would be about an abducted homeless man, how the culprits shave him with hundreds of tiny purple nicks, then paint him naked blue. This is an everyday danger everyday Americans face every day, notes the NRA. That's why we need to carry concealed blue notes. Note how we build multi-orgasmic stadiums to better surround our many selves with the clash of steroid-popping blue cows. On the last hour of the last day Bill Gates will trump open his electronic gates and let the herds of indeterminate blue cows mingle and murmur amongst us, who will be overjoyed and overstimulated unto forgetfulness to be so amongst.

INVOLVING THE USE OF THE WORD *AMERICA*

In America, Kafka began, and paused, staring at the peeling gray planks on the front porch. *In America,* he began again, but lost his way in the enormity of the phrase.

It was a sticky August day, but Kafka still wore his heavy gray overcoat and black bowler.

Would you like a beer? I asked, but he shook his head, pointing to his throat.

What would you say if the President of the United States came up to your front porch right now? Kafka asked, trying to be patient, *If he shook your hand and patted you on the back? What would you say?*

Offer him a beer?

Would you tell him how you ate your landlord because he stole your father's eyebrows? Would you tell him how your wife ran off with your uranium which you kept hidden in the valium? Would you tell him Jack Ruby is secretly transmitting coded messages through the letters turned by Vanna White?

Probably not.

No, this is America. You would, instead, ask for parrots, obscenely colored parrots, to be released from cornfields in Nebraska and Iowa and Ohio. Thousands of purple and yellow and green parrots. Isn't that what you really want?

I shrugged my shoulders. *Sounds all right to me, I guess.*

His face looked tight, sallow, like an egg boiled too long. If I took a spoon and broke open the egg, I knew what I would see—garishly colored parrots perched on televisions of all sizes strewn across a cornfield. And, when a parrot opened its beak, out would fly tiny felt parrots wearing black sombreros, with little bandoleers slung across their breasts. I sighed, my breath a sticky purple.

See? said Kafka, cleaning his nails with a switchblade, its handle a larger-than-normal sausage. *In America,* he began again, but lost his way in the enormity of the phrase.

THREE PRESIDENTS

I'm in line with a group of school kids granted a special visit with the President before his scheduled talk in front of the courthouse later that day. Each of the children gives President Reagan a gift. The kid in front of me strokes a hamster painted red, white, and blue. I notice, too late, that I have nothing to give the President. He frowns at the frayed cuffs of my blue jean jacket. I *used to be a paper boy, you know,* he tells me. Not knowing what else to do, I take off my jacket and gingerly hand it to him, as if it were made from the original copy of the Declaration of Independence. He shakes my hand. A few blocks away, a roving helicopter above me, I notice I'm wearing the blue jean jacket once again.

All set? says this guy with curly black hair and a red tie tucked inside his plaid shirt. I nod and follow Curly, one of the President's men or part of the camera crew, through the school cafeteria and outside, to the front of the one-story brick building. Two lounges recline in the sun before an arsenal of television equipment. Why did I ever agree to this in the first place? So my mother could tell her friends that I was the teacher selected by the President to discuss education issues on national tv? Curly leads me over to my lounge, tells me to "just relax," and then goes over to Clinton, who, by the other lounge, listens to an aid explain how the president's negatives have risen this week with families owning a handgun and a La-Z-Boy and an SUV. *Aren't you that teacher who got in trouble,* asks a head-phoned technician, *for using Monopoly to teach American history?*

A rest stop in Springfield, Illinois, in the mens room. Here, in the city of Honest Abe, Lincoln's face stares up at me from the bottom of the urinal. Pennies tossed into the constitutional wishing well.

PARABLE OF THE WHITE HOUSE REPLICA

I can still remember the day a cloud of ammonia covered the White House and I was called in to pull the President out of the bathtub. I eat a boiled egg and an unboiled egg each day to heighten my balance. It must be difficult to have to walk through the White House naked, even if they let you keep on your socks and shoes. I couldn't find anyone in the presidential bathtub, nothing except the mannequin leg, once worn by Martha Washington.

It was a good thing they had a spare copy of the President down the basement. All they had to do was send a few volts through him and he was waving his hand and signing his name to everything within reach. Sometimes I add a dash of powdered reindeer antlers to my eggs. Then I start singing "Don't Fence Me In." You can still see some of the presidential signature, if you look carefully, behind my right ear. Sort of looks like it says *Killallamoeba.*

Then the President's wife, or someone dressed like her, snuck in without paying to see the exhibit of the broccoli replica of the White House. It was no bigger than the harmonica used by Henry Kissinger when he played "Who Do You Love?" with Bo Diddley. Sometimes I eat just the boiled egg, but I make sure I eat a raw egg within the next forty-eight hours. I never wash behind my ears. I can't bear to erase our disappearing American history.

KILLARNEY CLARY

Killarney Clary is the author of four books of poetry, including *By Me, By Any, Can and Can't Be Done* (Greenhouse Review Press, 1980), *Who Whispered Near Me* (Noonday Press, 1990), *By Common Salt* (Oberlin College Press, 1996), and *Potential Stranger* (University of Chicago Press, 2003). She received a 1992 Lannan Foundation Fellowship in Poetry and lives in Los Angeles, California.

In this wind, the sharp blue cut of the San Gabriels flattens against the neon east; eucalyptus want to break loose but hold, thrashing, to what is. Just air, all air, all tossed and secured at once; and when I see I am in a dry room, listen to the flyer as its banded to the outer doorknob, I say, "here." But I am all pull.

I am walking in the arroyo. I am in love; I am scared. Everyone is still alive. The leaves aren't sad and restless; the canyon isn't cooling so fast, darkening between its walls as the days shorten and the way narrows. I am not going back. There is no body made to take me back into itself.

Always in the in-between, at ease with my tongue in its pool, or taking a shocking first breath in the bright room in the hands of an expert. Lucky, in-between, where friction finds me.

No one promised to go with me to Texas or the market, into the next hour here in Los Angeles where I've set the house plants on the porch so they won't be bored or suspect that the anxiety of stillness sucks up all options. As if they want. I had an idea that there is certainty, an object maybe, stone in my hand or sun on my face, but there's not a thing I would call real. No one coming with me toward the mountains, the streams of the forks of the San Gabriel River, on the crunch of dry ravel on the creature earth that lets me ride. All dream. Not even the itch or cut or blood from the cut or cold water on it, trout in a shadow, camouflage of reflection, or the leaves that fall to meet their pictures. Again I meet my picture and will not promise myself what lies there. Light off the moon as if there were a moon.

The man has lost his way in the snow and he prays, lies against a stone as he grows sleepier. In the shape of the branches above, what does he see that assures him? The light is weak; the edges of the picture dull.

What will be found when the snow melts? When the reservoir is drained? That quick shadow below the bridge has something pressing to tell about nearly effortless transformation.

I want to complete a deliberate action, make a single perfect offering. What will be left? I was once on both sides of a patch of sunlight on a baby's arm. Not mere memory, but attar.

A small stranger without edges I need this container of *please*. I turn, walk onto Ocotillo Mesa. Their squirrely arms reach up, tips aflame, a begging frenzy of thorns in a silent hundred degrees.

Offered endless fire they send up their own in return. Some sweet taste rises to meet sugar, and the best answer is a cast of the question. No one knows where I am.

El Paso. Eleventh floor of the hotel in a dust storm with eight hundred miles of interstate ten vibrating behind my eyes. Two nights ago there were two of us. East of Redlands, I was away, and couldn't remember or predict. There spun the windmill blades defiantly, making use.

I hear grains of grit tick against the glass and a howl that won't let up. No time to inhale. On point, I might fall cynical, fall sentimental; they are the same. I want you to stand in front of me and be other. The wall of umber air thins for a span and the city sharpens. I figure as I watch the depot sign dim and clear without pattern the number of interruptions, the shortest distance.

At junctures we renamed the roads for what happened there: Glasses Lost, Insult, Why Are There No Ghosts. We never returned to the places, and though our trackers felt they learned our history, the sequence was senseless. We could have faced nearly any direction, since what drove us was a desire to occur without erasing what we'd made.

We agreed. We were not scared; we wouldn't be caught. No children. We held hands in ceremony but were uneasy with it. We each had our own pack. We didn't even envy birds.

Would I dive again into ambient refulgence; try to prove there once was a paradise of amber, second in splendor only to the sun?

In advance of a scalding wall of ash, glass softened, the harbors boiled; or water rose through and then above the bogland. In any case, the continent was clean gone.

Relieved at familiar disappointment, I go under, susceptible to nitrogen narcosis, sure to be thoughtless and grand among the fry of invention: a sunken island west of the end of the known world.

Urchins plead from a kelp holdfast; drifters pump and trail. Below this depth, pressure replaces bones and muscle; direction is lost. I only want to help the fish breathe.

Pieces that jammed when forced, tore when pulled apart. Grit fell under fireworks and stars leaked through the smudge afterward. Bonfires leveed the procession of the palette upon which the statue danced. Body of pieces.

The dark crowd shifted and whirred. I put my hand on the stranger's back because we walked on ice—no surprise at my touch. Body of falling snow, of cinders, falling. Body of ashes. A dead man's reading glasses on a drain grate. A limp mantilla at the back of a drawer. What proof of an afterlife do we need? A vision burned into an old shirt.

Early on the day of the reception I lit new candles and extinguished them. The wicks were charred, the wax untouched. Ready.

The boy had told a rhyme as he unfastened his pants. He was scolded, ended up in the cab of a big rig with this man he slightly knew, under a clear sky on the straight desert interstate.

On the dock the driver and receiver agreed on the sky's shift, a cold front. Both were in shirt sleeves, laughing. Now the driver went back to the icy waiting room to fetch the boy. On the green vinyl chair he was propped, blood clotting at his mouth; he was shivering. The driver picked him up like an armful of tissue paper. I felt that. I felt his young feathery breath. "My poor boy," I moaned. I was lifted. I was light as a dried leaf, dried brittle star, headlights through falling snow. I was high above the road, traveling.

A truck pulled up. Footsteps on the gravel drive lagged at the windows. Two men in jeans and white T-shirts stooped at the faucet, talked a little; one fingered the dry threads. They worked surely, laughed as they stood, watered tufts of grass in the sandy soil.

With standard prayers thick in your bones, a dependable simplicity fortified, you answer me with what you want—a smile, Sunday afternoon.

Dishes I break and I watch them break. My project requires disorder, the sanctuary of replacing pieces. You cannot help me fix this. Erratic amen.

JON DAVIS

Jon Davis is a professor of creative writing at The Institute of
American Indian Arts in Santa Fe, New Mexico. A graduate
of The University of Montana, Davis has published three
chapbooks and two full collections of poetry, *Dangerous
Amusements* (Ontario Review Press, 1987) and *Scrimmage of
Appetite* (The University of Akron Press, 1995).

AN AMERICAN

"An American," Maximus wrote, "is a complex of occasions." And occasion—he would have known this—means to fall toward. To fall, as my wife and I fell, yesterday, toward coffee and a pleasant bookstore. As we fell, this morning, toward—in the local newspaper—a photograph of that bookstore. A photograph that must have been taken shortly before we arrived, that commemorates absence, that attends to everything not photographed—racks of magazines and books, crumbling adobe neighborhoods, telephone wires swaying with intense, casual conversations, memories swelling in the lilacs, flowing in the acequias, blood-spattered priests, jailed Pueblo leaders, cache of longing under the plaza grass, longing shaped into earrings and pottery, longing inscribed in racks of blankets, vested in theaters and galleries, scribbled in margins, entwined among arbors and portals. These Americans strolling the tax-sheltered streets of Santa Fe—*what is the real name of this place?*—are a complex of occasions. Are *falling,* and the photograph says, *Lovely.* And the photograph says, *Here is the generous life upwelling.* And the photograph says, *It is time to write the diary of your days. Among the gathered blossoms, in the morning courtyard, in the casual isolation you want to call privacy.*

BLUES

Forms seek subjects.
—Frank Bidart

The first line must be about heartbreak: "Oh, she stomped my heart / give me the stompin blues." The second must be the first sung with increasing rage and despair: "Yeah, she stomped my heart / gi' me the STOMPin blues." The third must add detail and complete the breakage: "She stomped it with my best friend/ wore my favorite shoes."

At this point, the guitar may complain or cry. At this point, the singer may moan, "Oh, baby." At this point, a white boy, a construction laborer in work boots and flannel shirt may, having been overcome by the poignancy of the occasion and several draught beers, begin to sway and shout "Amen!" thrusting his plastic cup into the air.

Which may or may not signal the coming of an avant-garde. Say the next time he shouts, "Radiator!" Say the next time he shouts, "Come unto the Lord." Say the next time he shouts, "I'm on fire" or "Stuff the turkey. The kids are in the car and I can't stay long." Say he talks over the bridge, saying, "The cake flopped. The cake flopped. We gave it to the cousin who eats such things."

Say he begins rocking vigorously and continues: "The linoleum's cracking by the fridge. When the welfare lady comes be neat, be clean, but don't be happy. Tell her we never have enough. Tell her we behave anyway. After dark, if we lean the brick palette against the back wall and climb it like a ladder and pull ourselves onto the back porch where the door is always open, we can go inside."

At this point, the guitarist may attack a single note and hold it. "We'll bring a flashlight—a small one—and we'll eat ice cream and cheese and steal the records—Love, Steppenwolf, *The Soft Parade, Dr. Byrd and Mr. Hyde.* When I call your brand of cigarettes, the brand you're thinking of, you run around the yard and I'll try to catch you. Darkness. Toads along the porch. Katydids creaking. Bats. One night we shined a flashlight into the maple and watched small animals hurl themselves onto the roof of the house. Flying squirrels."
He might also mention the way those bats flew—the veering, the way they swooped at the stones he tossed. The stones he gathered from the driveway where the Dugan man parked his bread truck. It would be nearly dark, and he'd climb in the open door with his brothers and eat cherry pies while the Dugan man

drank coffee with his grandmother. Then they'd slip out the side door and the bars would be veering above.

Attraction and avoidance. This is the blues. It keeps repeating itself. Keeps repeating its lonesome self. The object is purgation. Catharsis. The object is triumph. Endurance. Humor. At this point, the singer may shout, "Hurt me!" And the guitar may answer, *Pain, pain, pain. Pain, pain, pain.*

THE SORRY PART

This is "the sorry part" and the father is laughing. The girl, who has tormented the boy and the boy's family. The angry, the *single-minded* sister. The too-handsome. The witty. The self-involved. All, in an instant, transformed. Insight already shaping itself into the florid Latinates of confession and forgiveness. The inwardness displayed on the screen, the signs of inwardness, the training grown crucial and apparent, the eyes cast down, the timing, oh, the timing. This is the sorry part and the father is laughing—*who does he think he is?*

For an hour, the family has watched, together, the plot unscrolling. For an hour, minus the numerous other minutes blossoming with products and the pantheon of imagery—flowers, endangered species, muscles, and sweat in this age of lives measured backward from absence.

For an hour, the family has endured the thoughtless, the captive of Beverly Hills, wandering through their inane traumas—kiss, sleep, banish some other from one's life, wash cars, build a float for some parade celebrating banality, phone calls, some Puccini played with mock passion on a small stage, then gasoline poured dramatically on something they were supposed to want preserved, some *property*.

For an hour, and, now, this is the sorry part. The past, suppressed so long, wriggles up like a frog out of the mud, blinking its eyes. The past with its cliched bellowing. The past with its eloquent soliloquies. The past with its arm in a sling. With its mazes where the lost children keep wandering, creating a kind of gyroscope that assures the orbit of their lives will be erratic, elliptical.

This is the sorry part, the five-year-old says. She knows this part. She has lain in bed and heard how these stories unfold.

First the mother speaks sharply, then the father shouts, then both grow silent. Time passes, during which she sleeps and dreams of dragons and ducks.

Then the long, earnest conversation which is music with duration and timbre but without melody. Doors slammed at intervals. At intervals, the brass of complaint and amelioration. Then birds singing and a light in the trees. Soon, then, the sorry part.

One must not laugh. The birds are singing. The earth is rolling like a whale in a calm sea, letting the sun wash over its gray flanks. There will be speeches or there will be no speeches. The script is meaningless. This is form and drama. First the man and woman love each other and then the man and woman love each other. In between, they stare at the window expecting darkness bur see instead their own watery, ineffable forms.

One must not laugh. One must lie in bed and wait. One must rise seriously and slip down the hall, bare feet on stone—the slapping sounds of bare feet hurrying on stone—to press the bedroom door open, walk in and stand, poised in morning sunlight and the certainties of form.

THE SIXTIES: TWO SCENES

1. In the Church / 4th of July / Derby, Connecticut

Once the mercury flowed in Danbury and found the river down there. The children kept climbing the hills. Kept sliding back down. Posters, papers, incense. Stoned and adrift on the water bed. Wine in a paper bag. A park full of promise. When they finally sent the police in. Whose children were they? He carried his flute everywhere he went. The door to the church was open. Someone blew every candle out. The light from the parking lot glowed against the stained-glass windows. Flute song like torn wind. Like a flame. Anything could happen. The man on the cross kept opening his arms. The Grand Finale was about to begin. Flute song. Flute song. Detonations through the church walls.

2. Listening

Standing on the lake. Winter. There were more drugs in there, he said. His eyes kept trying to escape his face. Later, he would live with cows in Massachusetts. Would work in a pickle factory. Later he would live in a hole in the ground. All winter, he said, digging deeper when it got cold, sliding the darkness over his head. Here is the sun, dazzling the lake. Surfaces full of presence. Hendrix wanted us all to. Hendrix kept appearing in the form of smoke. The world was frozen over. Later, on an oil rig in Texas, the boom would thump his head and the medical team would suspect a brain lesion. Hendrix, he'd whisper to the spinning record, what do you want from us?

IN HISTORY

The room was an emblem for loneliness—no toast in the toaster, blinds carefully parted. One finger, tugging. The neighborhood was full of strangers. He recognized that. They argued in front of, no, behind their picture windows. The bullet would have already entered, piercing the newly reupholstered davenport. No: *couch*. That was the name history had found for it. "Late in the Twentieth Century there was a great spiritual awakening." Announcers on some channels kept saying that. It was a voice-over while the many well-groomed Americans looked skyward. Later, they would play the Super Bowl. Everyone had to watch or be left speechless at break time. The man entered the woman from behind. Later, they would pass a law. He couldn't help feeling that objects were pressing up against his eyes. He tried to push them away. If he could have painted what he saw. If he could have written it down. The crowd was cheering in unison. In unison, they wanted the quarterback dead or maimed.

Outside, a building rose until it filled the window. There were no shots. Not yet. But he couldn't help feeling he had caused them. He had wanted to move the couch. To hang the Monet on the wall above the stereo. He had wanted to obliterate his feelings. Quit his job. Burn the house. He had wanted to place a single rose in a thin, crystal bud vase. He muted the television with the remote. The woman moaned a little; he whimpered, grateful. Opening his eyes, he saw the building, people slapping hands: 49er fans. *Gold rush.* History was incomprehensible. Intolerable. The blinds were barely parted. The bullet already tearing through fabric, the cotton batting splashing around the bullet. An emblem of his sickness. He should kiss her afterward. He should explain himself to the dust motes circulating in the afternoon light. But she was gone. He was listening to the Pentagon spokesman: "Bomb damage assessment is an art, not a science." He wondered about the implication of this confusion. And why did he think of it now? We leave him there, wondering. We resist his attempts to draw us into the puzzle. He leans to touch the already unscarred fabric.

THE WHEEL OF APPETITE

What should the birds mean, huddled in the eaves as the wind stretches its story over the yard? As the dust hums of barrenness to the grass? As darkness sets up its filigreed tent? Why does the raven peer into our rooms and shrug? Or tumble from flight as if shot? An omen or the predictable loopings of chaos? The patternlessness that achieves elegance only in distance or memory. Like our lives.

When my friend left her husband the night seemed full of a purple sheen that kept drawing itself out of the darkest corners. The future kept snapping at her, snarling and hissing and backing into its hole. All the lies she'd carefully assembled shifted beneath her. Trust was a paper boat she'd floated on an ocean. No sentence could accommodate her despair. *I am no one, I am no one,* she sang. She was eighteen she was forty. The years were an ellipsis she could not complete.

What was missing? Two cars, a house, enough furniture to seat their several friends. Shades to thwart the curious. Food and a dish to slide under it. Figurines and paintings they'd shopped their weekends for. Emblems of togetherness, their compromises, extremes. Already emptied of their histories, assertions and passions, their tenderness. His records, her books. The unstrung guitar, the unpainted canvas. The yearly hobbies abandoned in the attic. The self-help books glowering and cajoling from the nightstand. The television bristling and crackling in the darkened room, speaking of failure to the unconverted.

The bitten nails, the lost argument of the flesh. A device to strap across the stomach's drowse, a system of filters and conduits to divert the elegant, poisonous smoke from the lungs. The trained kindnesses and seductive hands. The latest disease and its expensive cure. The groomed finger of light pointing out her failure to achieve happiness. She could snap it off from any point in her den. She could watch the shadow slide across the adobe wall. Or was the light failing?

And what of the finches? They hopped oblivious along the wall, chattering of nothing to the air. The bright reddishness at their throats gave a momentary pleasure each time she drank it, but the meaninglessness terrified her. In each mouth, a bit of straw for the nest. Each bird, an appetite with wings. They mated indiscriminately, closeting their young in the junipers. None feared routine or flew resolutely into the bumpers of cars. None dropped the straw to elope with the promise of continual ease and delight.

Ease and continual delight. Here were the recipes, the spring fashions, the CD with its strummed guitars and its new song about loneliness and the failures of language. Here was the new movie about dying. A dance to make us look like machines; a machine to make us look like dancers. A device to obliterate the meadowlark's song, the wind's idiotic duet with the cottonwoods.

The wheel of appetite spins like a gyroscope in our groins. In our stomachs and eyes. From the first apple to the glittering Porsche. But to sit among the piñon and sage. To let the wind blow and dust settle on the skin and not think of erosion and death, of loss and stillness and the closets of our unhappiness. To watch the scrub jays hurtle across the open spaces and lodge in the thick fur of the piñons and not see them as evil but as embodiments of a singular, fierce, and manageable appetite.

THE HAWK. THE ROAD. THE SUNLIGHT AFTER CLOUDS.

Say you are driving in Vermont, spring, the sun emerging from clouds, the road twisting among farmhouses and farmhouses converted into country homes for the wealthy, and a bird breaks out of the woods into the air above and just in front of your car, startles, catches himself, spreads his rufous wings and his broadly striped tail and becomes a hawk, a broad-winged hawk.

You have been driving five hours and, until this moment, have deadened yourself with the radio's ragged rock—a half-dozen chords and the lyrics: "I love her but now she's shopping with him," "The refrigerator's open and the beer is gone." Some cross between pleasure and pain where noise meets noise: the guitar's doodle and thwack, the tires' rabble, the whistle from the window that won't quite shut.

You are leaving a place where you could not quite make a living, heading to a place where you will not quite make a living. You are, of course, me. You (here I mean you) are probably relieved to be out of that car, although you can, if you were born in America at midcentury, no doubt recall being in similar circumstances.

I am writing this for you, though I hope others—Mexicans, Swedes, Egyptians, Americans of future and past generations—can also imagine driving a car, seeing a bird, a hawk, a small hawk not ten feet away through the windshield, beautiful the way it catches itself, acknowledging your presence by veering slightly.

I want you to see this because seeing it myself is meaningless, lonely. I don't want to be alone in my seeing. Though the sight lightened me, somehow, made me forget the pains in my back, the dull throbbing in my temples. And it was a way of keeping time, of remembering: The Trip Before the Hawk / The Trip After the Hawk.

Still, it must seem a trivial thing to those struggling with arid land, government oppression. But I can imagine the sight of a bird lightening even those burdens. The right bird in the right place—aloft and weightless or nearby, perched. The different meanings there. Robins roosting or gulls drifting. My year-old daughter watches the crows and gulls returning to roost at dusk. "Bird," she says, tapping the glass. "Bird."

And I suspect that Noah's dove was notable not because it carried an olive branch, but simply because it was a bird, aloft, the freedom it promised the captives of the crowded, rocking ark, the hope embodied there, the feeling of hope, how we are lightened by hope, how even the soul seems to be birdlike—winged and able to sing.

Can you understand this, withering mothers and children, South Africans, Salvadorans, you there starving, you sealed in the box in darkness, you with your genitals wired to the generator? I saw this bird and it made me feel better. I just wanted to tell you about it. Can you imagine my freedom?

I was driving, yes *driving* from one state to another. My wife was in another car. Yes, we had two cars. We stopped to eat twice. My daughter was smiling at strangers. Can you imagine that? Now I am sitting on the porch of a lakeside cottage. I can see everyone, and everyone can see me and I am utterly safe. I am making a list of the birds I see:

> black-throated blue warbler
>
> phoebe
>
> barn swallow
>
> northern oriole
>
> crow

I have a little money, some food, and this house I'm renting. I have read some history. There are always wars. There are always two literatures—the literature of the oppressor, the literature of the oppressed. The literature of the oppressor is always stylistically superior (he has more time); the literature of the oppressed is always more urgent (he has less time).

Rain falls gently on the lake; the coffee cools at my elbow. Across the water, a man cuts logs with a chainsaw. Above my head, nestling phoebes faintly chirp their hunger songs. Once, I was driving in Vermont and a hawk hung briefly over the hood of my car. It was beautiful—the hawk, the road, the sunlight after clouds.

I have written about that hawk, about seeing that hawk. In the days to come I will write about similar incidents: the small joys and miseries, the tribulations of love in a privileged society, the speckled flanks of a brook trout, the things my daughter says. Wouldn't you? Given the time and freedom. Wouldn't you?

BRUTAL SQUARES

The poem arrives emblazoned in language. The poem arrives festooned with rhythm and a sense of completion. It is half of the rainbow. The rainbow slowly materializing. The rainbow that grew until it touched the meadows beside the river. The rainbow that my daughter and I followed until it fell, barely visible—a sheen, a radiance—around the black and white cows grazing disconsolately beside the mud-engorged Pecos River. Augury, therefore. The poem a dry lake. Words like water. And the big beat—rock 'n' roll, the metronomic swings of the moon, tidal pulse. And the child's epistemology: *Because.* The navigable, the *companionable,* world. Father sun, mother earth, and the story told in many cultures of the sun's penis. The Ojibwa story of the woman impregnated by the sun. In the fields, among the unfurling leaves.

But this dream takes place in the brutal squares, in the hard pan, in the terror-inflected markets. Southeast Asia and the pages of history flutter in a dry wind. In a dream, and two men emerge like lungfish from drought. Memory cracks the mud-crust of daily life. Inside, the war-scarred child. Inside, in the moment preserved like a diamond of pain. Inside, the ochre world. Inside, sunlight and shadow. But the men want clarity. The men want certainty. The men want, therefore, death. Which is the usual, the order of the day. A clear winner. They torment each other with their own disappointments. *You,* they are saying. *You live in a golden light and are untouched by beauty.*

Meanwhile, the crows. Meanwhile, the world's desolate clarity. Meanwhile, the woman. Her back arched as if. In memory, *into* memory, into *language. In language—where desire swims with just its eyes showing.* Meanwhile, outside the sentence. Meanwhile, color and festival. Meanwhile, the sun, the big beat. Woodstock, and Hendrix returning the anthem into the poisonous air of its birth. Notes swirl in the rich farmland. *In an ochre world—*two men, veterans, veterans of violence and anger, veterans of what the Romanian poet, in a seminar, called "the occult workings of governments." If they cannot have the world they want, they want no world. *Because.* And the corn and squash. And the world saying, *live.* And the world saying, *in memory, the red balloon, the woman.* Listen: *This anger is deep and so is joy.*

MEMORY

The radio is playing John Lennon's "Imagine" and I have to stand and walk around the room because walking is a defense against feeling, the past, memory. Is a way of swimming when the past washes over and tries to fill the lungs. But there is no defense against memory.

I remember walking in Provincetown, the air thinned by an approaching storm, how the sand and gravel underfoot sounded poignant, and how to explain that? The harbor kept its surf and sadness to itself. The highway was a secret only the eye could unfold.

Listen: I mean to tell you for no good reason how it felt to walk that night alone going on lonely, considering physics: how sound moves through air, the way a rock's vibrations move through water, whether these sounds my feet kept making were stronger than the same sounds on a clear day and what other differences. I was thinking about timbre, how a sort of hollowness—foghorn at night, merest rustlings of a dry oak leaf, a woman's footsteps on the stairs— could stir my body or bring me near tears.

It's not the brain or the mind or something the ear knows how to do. It's not the body making its own rules. It's not memory alone or the present with its fistful of facts, but the way memory reaches out with its little arms and weary voice: "Don't leave me here. I have been waiting for someone to get me out of this house, walk me to the bus stop, ride with me though there is nowhere to go."

I'm speaking of hollowness, the richness of something with something missing—dry riverbed, abandoned nest, the promise that is not a promise, scrape of boot against sand in the lee of a storm. Because memory is a hollow in the body. Because memory is an animal, a sad, furry thing curled in that hollow.

I am thinking of that family in Brazil who found a radioactive canister and took it home because they'd been waiting for it forever and didn't know it. Who placed it on the table and watched. Because it was beautiful and seemed a gift from the gods. Because now, finally, they had it.

I know what you're thinking: That canister is a metaphor for nothing. People were maimed and killed and it was real. Forgive me. I am placing this canister on the table. It is memory and throws a terrible light. Now the body will pour out all of its beauty and grace. Now, unable to bear it, I will stand and walk around this room.

THE BAIT

This is not an elegy because the world is full of elegies and I am tired of consoling and being consoled. Because consolation is unsatisfying and even tenderness can do nothing to stop this loss, this dying, this viciousness among men.

And god just complicates, offering justice like the cracker I place on this mouse trap. Then frantic mouse hands pushing against the metal bar, kicking and bucking, the fall from the shelf, more kicking, one eye bulging, lips lifted and the little yellowed teeth clamped on the small crumb of goodness that was not goodness but something alluring and, finally, dumb—without equivalent in the human world. Just food he couldn't have.

My food and what that means in the scale of human affairs. I didn't want to listen to this mouse scrabbling among the graham crackers, chewing into the can of grease, leaving a trail of greasy, orange, rice-like shits in the cabinet under the sink. I didn't want to clean those up every morning; I didn't want to be awakened in the night.

I set the trap; the trap smashed his skull; he kicked awhile and he died. I tossed him, trap and all, into the dunes. But I was saying something about god and justice. I was saying this is not an elegy and why. Because pain is the skin we wear? Because joy is that skin also?

Because...look: I had a brother and he died. I didn't cause it; I couldn't stop it. He got on his motorcycle and rode away. A car turned in front of him and that began his dying. How terrible for everyone involved. Do I sound bitter? I felt the usual guilts: Did I love him enough. Did I show it.

It happened eleven years ago and what I remember: Looking out at the lawn, September and a breeze; watching him ride—flash of red gas tank, brown leather jacket; the sound of the bike; what we said, which I recall as a kind of gesture, the sound of *what are you doing,* some dull rhythm and *see you later.*

The phone call. The drive to the hospital. I think I drove bur I can't be sure. We drove the wrong way down a one-way street and I remember feeling responsible. I cried most of the time. I knew he was dying. My brother's girlfriend asked me *Why are you crying?* and I couldn't say or else I sobbed *It's bad I know it's bad.*

Then we were taken into a green room and told he was dead. I curled on a red plastic chair. My body disappeared or seemed to. I was looking for my brother; a nurse called me back: *Your family needs you.* I came back.

But why am I telling you this? Because I want you to love me? To pity me? To understand I've suffered and that excuses my deficiencies? To see how loss is loss and no elegy, no quiet talk late at night among loved ones who suddenly feel the inadequacy of their love and the expression of that love can take it away? Or give it back? Perhaps even loss is lost?

My brother is gone and the world, you, me, are not better for it. There was no goodness in his death. And there is none in this poem, eleven years later and still confused. An attempt, one might say, to come to terms with his death as if there were somewhere to come to, as if there were terms. But there is nowhere to come to; there are no terms. Just this spewing of words, this gesture neither therapy nor catharsis nor hopelessness nor consolation. Not elegy but a small crumb. An offering.

LINDA DYER

Linda Dyer received an MFA in Creative Writing from Warren Wilson College and has been the recipient of fellowships from The Colorado Council on the Arts, The NeoData Endowment for the Humanities, and the Vermont Studio Center. She is the author of a collection of poetry, *Fictional Teeth* (Ahsahta Press, 2001) and lives in San Francisco.

HEREDITARY GUESS

I come from a long line of drunkards and cheats. My mother touched the oil paintings in museums explaining symbol to us, explaining style. My father pocketed artifacts from the Petrified Forest while the mounted guards surveyed the valley in another direction. My cousin draws police sketches, composites of criminals, all made to look like his father. My brother lights candles without dropping coins in the box. Me? I steal my own memories so they can't be used for profit or loss. My sister, in her diary, asks God to show her a sign, to rearrange the ashes in the fireplace. How do I know? I read the secrets in diaries, an averted gaze, a furtive reaching for something concealed in the hand.

VOTIVE

Being rural, we waited for the schoolbus in the dark early morning of daylight savings, then proceeded to the subdivisions. On our bus in 1972, it was unpopular to wear a "Vote McGovern" button, to carry a clarinet case, to read books on the ride. What a relief to focus on a battle outside the home, stand up for our man McGovern, believe the forces of liberal overspill would help out when Bobby Hawkins pushed you up against the graffiti wall and told you to take it back. *Take back McGovern. Say you vote Nixon.* All this for weeks of obsessive campaigning for something which might invade even our lone house with humankindness, bring us back to the fold, any fold—all of us too young to vote or influence our parents. Vindication was ours a few years later with "*I am not a crook* and the guilty swaggering, a few convictions; but in the '70s, rural Oklahoma, we were commies and queers, relegated to sitting in the library again for the lunch hour, our brown bag lunches confiscated in the name of Nixon.

FARM MUTILATIONS

The woman's fingers sheared off by the thresher at an angle, just leaving the wedding band intact. How did the truncated hand feel when smoothing her daughter's hair, resting in her husband's hand to dance?

The man trying to bring electricity to his barn, on the ladder, electrocuted when the wire touches his wedding ring. His teeth spill out, but he recovers.

My grandfather's ring finger caught in a door, cut off finally to release him. Not a farm story, but a working man's story which carried a shadowy metaphor in our family ever since. See what trouble a ring can get you into—the drinking, the odd jobs, the food baskets left on the doorstep for the long-suffering wife and seven children.

THE LOST FINGER

Before he was "ex," my husband told me about his father making a boat for him, and as he was guiding the wood he left his hand too close to the blade of the saw: little finger gone! How the father made the boy take a cigarette out of his pocket, put it in his mouth and light it. Then they could look for the finger and someone to do something about it. The point was, my ex-husband had pestered his father about making the boat and later when he started using swear words and his father died, it was the same set-up. And wasn't it much the same as what he and I did to each other because after all he was right to want the boat, to want his father to make it for him and for them to sail it together, if indeed it could float. The lost finger and the boat never finished, the table-saw sold at a garage sale and then the cursing, death, later the marriage which produced no children, no property, and little more than a few stories we used to tell about the other's childhood as if we had been there but better because we could embellish or impoverish it for our guests as the feeling between us demanded—the story, for instance, of how his father stuck the stub of his finger into his nostril so it looked like a finger was emerging from his nose and how after a few times the boy was embarrassed, though his father was a good example, don't you think, to turn his losses into humor?

When I left, I said I'd never fallen in love with him, and it was true, but didn't say that later when the next love was over. After all, doesn't working hard make up for absent passion, doesn't working long at it make up for a hasty decision? Last night I had a dream about his forearm, the underside of it, and thought fondly of him though not without maternal overtones. I missed him as I might miss a child I wanted who didn't belong to me but who I'd take to the zoo and the movies, so that now on an overcast Sunday I might think of him as I make a pot of strong tea and drink half.

FIRST DEATH IN OKLAHOMA

In French class, my boyfriend thought the French word for Saturday *(Samedi)* sounded like "suck my dick" said really fast. It was all we could do to say it straight-faced to Madame Anderson. *Jeudi, Vendredi, Samedi*—and then, there he is, my early love, unfurled and durable, suited up in a casket with a message on his lips, a furtive pun. And here it is, Saturday.

WELLSPRING

"After the eighth child, you just can't get your figure back!" she said, now up to 12 births and full-bellied, though not from food. So unfull, in fact, that when the family dog knocked over the butter churn, ruining the contents on the dirt floor, she took him by the collar and hung him in the live oak where he howled and died. No one spoke of it then, or until she was senile and arthritic, since the yellow dog was replaced with many other mutts, spoiled and hand-fed, sleeping with the children. Swift justice, the noose and dog cut down, but an end of rope still circling a tree in Nebraska, by way of Minnesota, the Netherlands, some old world of hunger and industry.

THE LIFE OF THE BODY

1.

Snails sleep in pairs to keep warm so they'll last the winter, though a child might give just one to her grandfather, who knows about their sleeping in pairs the way you would like us to do. These days I'm not drawn to you in the flesh, only in memory, and anger is dismantling even that until I read your letters again and think of burning them; but this is a high-pollution day and I might be arrested by the authorities who are working to reduce the brown cloud because it's a detriment to tourism. After the volcano erupted, for a long time, people wore masks just to breathe on the street and baby carriages were covered with hard plastic shields so a sleeping infant's lungs might be spared.

2.

When we go to hitchhike home we can't find a ride and walk all the way to Angel Fire before a green Cadillac stops and we slide over the leather seats and I fall asleep in air conditioning for the short way to Eagle Nest. Then more walking back to the Boy Scout Ranch and kitchen duty: shining the stainless steel doors to the walk-in refrigerators, pouring hot water into the trays under pans of food. There will be plums in heavy syrup for dinner. I will smile in my hairnet and serve you ⁱ of a spoonful of potatoes and pass your tray along the line where you pay at the end. For those of us who work here, food is a necessary encouragement to the body, not designed for pleasure but to keep us moving like machinery in the bright world, so on our days off we can create a few dark places out of it.

3.

I notice, as I go to put it in my mouth, mold inside the raspberry and wonder how much I've eaten already of the gray fungus which attaches itself and grows there. Like eating mushrooms: most are delicious, some deadly. Since I don't know how to tell the difference, I avoid them all. Irresistible deception: why we want what we want, and convince ourselves we are doing the right thing in the moment after a decision—to usher ourselves into believing *it is good, it is the only way.* Blessed are we who can verify our goodness by the power of our very testimony; like an echo returning, our voices sound like god answering back.

4.

When my father walked into a shoe shop in China to have a pair made the shoemaker laughed and laughed and held up his biggest last, many inches smaller than my father's foot. No Chinese shoes for him or his kind. My father's mother, all her life, jimmied her feet into stiff shoes several sizes too small so that her flesh rose out of the tops like loaves of bread. Even these smaller shoes were large for a woman, though. She had to shop in a special store in Germantown to find her size, which wasn't really her size, but what she preferred to see herself in.

LEVEL AND RISE

A satellite determines that sea level is overtaking the coast in relation to the polar caps melting, as refrigerators surge on and cars idle at the toll. Like a craving, I want to go to Alcatraz before it is submerged.

The men in solitary confinement heard revelers' voices on New Year's Eve, lilting into their disbelief once a year. In the solitude of my childhood, the quiet would wake me to check the body, and then I'd think of a new category to count myself to sleep: recite the names of my 67 cousins, the make of every cigarette and car, every song using the word blue, how the shelves were arranged at Sol's Drugstore, constellation of freckles on my mother's body, the order of my teeth falling out and the jagged permanent replacements.

One prisoner threw a button in the air, spun himself until he fell, then groped the floor for the button, all day. Or all night, it was the same; he knew how to fall without injury, and could feel time pass by the bruises and swellings which could be felt, but not seen, in the breathing dark.

THE SEVEN ANXIETIES OF SLEEP

i.

Staying up all night is the best that can be done:
hallucinogenic, cheap and adequate.

ii.

She had a crush on the church deacon (both on the narrow path, unbetrothed),
but when she told him of her interest (folklorious prohibition), he made her
understand it was not "of God." Despite his refusal, she continued in the choir,
girl that she was: overweight, unsure, with a lovely alto voice, neck splotched with
shame. Hadn't he appeared to her in a dream? Hadn't someone?

iii.

Her mom at the movies for the first time in years, laughing, commenting on every
scene, her cheeks indented by new eyeglasses on a smaller-than-average face,
glasses which will still be in place when she nods off in bed holding a cigarette.

iv.

Cogitation.

THE HARPIST, BETWEEN THE BEGINNING AND END

An old gag in Tommy Dorsey's band: let the light swing over to the harpist during a song; they've given her some fake knitting to pretend she's amusing herself in between the beginning and the end. My Aunt Nancy got the bigger laugh when she didn't fake it and actually knitted a 20-foot scarf. In Ricky Ricardo's band on the "I Love Lucy" show, her harp was so shiny she had to be moved to the back. Funny, gorgeous Aunt Nancy, who drank at home but never failed to put dinner on the table for her husband and two sons. As musicians go, she'd made it in Hollywood, town of the martini, and died of cirrhosis at 44.

A star and signal expert on the radio says (as he discusses the certainty of intelligent life in other galaxies) that, for example, "I Love Lucy" has reached 5,000 stars already. About one new star per day can tune in to the first episode; 6,000 Lucyfied stars by 2001.

My own mother's drinking, more excessive and disorderly, has been mysteriously slower in its destruction; she's outlived her sister by nearly 20 years. Seven musical sisters, one gone, all of us descendants with sad confessions, tapping quiet feet, listening for the notes that give us ten measures to get ready for a final glissando, and the stretched silence before the musicians lower their instruments and exhale.

RUSSELL EDSON

Russell Edson is the author of several collections of poetry, including *The Tormented Mirror* (University of Pittsburgh Press, 2001), *The Tunnel: Selected Poems* (Oberlin College Press, 1994), *Tick Tock* (Coffee House Press, 1992) and *The Reason Why the Closet-Man is Never Sad* (Wesleyan, 1977). He lives in Connecticut with his wife, Frances.

A MAN WHO MAKES TEARS

There was a man who made things because he was lonely. And so he made tears, which he thinks are tiny examples of the mystery that is large enough at times to swallow whole ships, and to be the road of the great whales....

The man makes tears which he thinks come out of his eyes from the memory of ponds and oceans. And he thinks they are the tears of a marionette whose head is a jug of water with a sad face painted on it....

THE DARK SIDE OF THE MOON

When a man returned he saw that everything had been melted, puddled flat. His fedora looked like a large rare coin. The dead moth on the window sill looked like a brown cloth draped from the window sill. The lamp on the night table looked like a fried egg...

He went to ask his landlady about all this melting, but found that even she was melted; on the floor like a wall-to-wall picture of the moon; one breast the Sea of Tranquillity, one eye the Sea of Opticus...

He looked for the vulva, and not finding it, decided it must be on the dark side of the moon...

THE LOVER

The lover has four legs and it loves itself the hairy pits of its arms and legs.

The lover has four arms and sleeps all tangled in its persons, all hands on skin and up backside through hair up belly a handful of breast the neck is sweet and the ear is kissed and the eye is kissed and the mouth licked.

And then sick of it all and a bird sings and the wallpaper hums with the monotony of a flower who is monotonous all over the walls.

The lover is two having coffee midsummer by a window, nude white ones in afternoon light full of twigs, a tree by the window.

CONJUGAL

A man is bending his wife. He is bending her around something that she has bent herself around. She is around it, bent as he has bent her.

He is convincing her. It is all so private.

He is bending her around the bedpost. No, he is bending her around the tripod of his camera.

It is as if he teaches her to swim. As if he teaches acrobatics. As if he could form her into something wet that he delivers out of one life into another.

And it is such a private thing the thing they do.

He is forming her into the wallpaper. He is smoothing her down into the flowers there. He is finding her nipples there. And he is kissing her pubis there.

He climbs into the wallpaper among the flowers. And his buttocks move in and out of the wall.

THE GLANDULAR CONDITION

After going through an inventory of names they decided to name their daughter Testicle after one of father's glands. And since Testicle had a twin sister they thought to call her Testicle too, after another of father's glands.

After that father had run out of glands.

Let us rejoice our four testicles, it's a miracle, said father.

Four? said mother.

My glands and their namesakes.

Are you trying to be disgusting?

Surely you've noticed my glandular condition? It's been described in several anatomical studies, and even sculpted in stone...

THE MARIONETTES OF DISTANT MASTERS

A pianist dreams that he's hired by a wrecking company to ruin a piano with his fingers…

On the day of the piano wrecking concert, as he's dressing, he notices a butterfly annoying a flower in his window box. He wonders if the police should be called. Then he thinks maybe the butterfly is just a marionette being manipulated by its master from the window above.

Suddenly everything is beautiful. He begins to cry.

Then another butterfly begins to annoy the first butterfly. He again wonders if he shouldn't call the police.

But, perhaps they are marionette-butterflies? He thinks they are, belonging to rival masters seeing whose butterfly can annoy the other's the most.

And this is happening in his window box. The Cosmic Plan: Distant Masters manipulating minor Masters who, in turn, are manipulating tiny butterfly-Masters who, in turn, are manipulating him…A universe webbed with strings!

Suddenly it is all so beautiful; the light is strange…Something about the light! He begins to cry…

THE WHEEL

A mother awoke her son and said, go down and hurt your father.

Can't I do it tomorrow? I was just having a dream in which I was revenging myself against you, he said.

You can dream tomorrow, the mother said.

So the son went down and tied a wagon wheel to his father's neck. I am not a vehicle, get this dirty thing off of me, said the father, for as you see I am writing a history of your mother.

The son yawned and went upstairs again.

He heard his father below: Get this wheel away from me quickly, as his father crawled with the wheel dragging from his neck. He heard his father scream: I do not want to write the history of the Wheel...Get this wheel away from me or I shall not be responsible for its safety.

Help help help, I cannot get away from a wheel. A wheel drives me crazy. A wheel has spokes which ray out of the hub to the rim. Help, I am beginning to fall in love with a wheel—I court a wheel because a wheel is to be courted—I marry a wheel—We live happily ever after.

Help help, I cannot get away from a wheel.

The son heard his father sighing: I am set out with a wheel. I go down the road with a wheel. I do not ride a wheel, I drag it because it will not stand up, as it is enraptured with me as my wife is not; that it clings to my neck as I crawl through the dust of the road.

THE FAMILY MONKEY

We bought an electric monkey, experimenting rather recklessly with funds carefully gathered since grandfather's time for the purchase of a steam monkey.

We had either, by this time, the choice of an electric or gas monkey.

The steam monkey is no longer being made, said the monkey merchant.

But the family always planned on a steam monkey.

Well, said the monkey merchant, just as the wind-up monkey gave way to the steam monkey, the steam monkey has given way to the gas and electric monkeys.

Is that like the grandfather clock being replaced by the grandchild clock?

Sort of, said the monkey merchant.

So we bought the electric monkey, and plugged its umbilical cord into the wall.

The smoke coming out of its fur told us something was wrong.

We had electrocuted the family monkey.

talking about something else through this odd, detached metaphor

consumeristic desires

TWINS

Identical twin old men take turns at being alive.

One stays in bed all day, dead. The other eats a cracker; then goes to the bathroom and evacuates the eaten cracker. He brushes his hair with a toothbrush.

If someone knocks on the door he opens it and says, hello, may I help you?

Then the person who knocked says, no, I don't think so.

But no one knocks...

The next day it's the dead old man's turn to be alive. So he gets up and eats a cracker, then goes to the bathroom to evacuate the cracker.

He brushes his hair with a toothbrush.

If someone knocks on the door he trembles.

But no one knocks on the door, so he doesn't tremble...

At dawn he dies, and it's his twin brother's turn to be alive again...

ROUND

When there is no shape there is round. Round has no shape; no more than a raindrop or a human tear…

And though the organs that focus the world are round, we have never been happy with roundness; how it allows no man to rest. For in roundness there is no place to stop, since all places in roundness are the same.

Thus the itch to square something. To make a box. To find proportion in a golden mean…

AMY GERSTLER

Amy Gerstler is the author of several books of poetry,
including *Medicine* (2000) and *Crown of Weeds* (1998), both
from Penguin. *Bitter Angel* (North Point Press, 1990) received
a National Book Critics Circle Award in Poetry in 1991. Her
writings on art have appeared in *Artforum* magazine and in
catalogs of exhibitions at the Long Beach Museum of Art,
the Los Angeles Museum of Contemporary Art, and the
Whitney Museum of American Art. She is a graduate adviser
at Art Center College of Design in Pasadena, California and
teaches in the graduate writing program at Antioch West
in Los Angeles.

DIFFICULTY AT THE BEGINNING

A shadow falls across the lap of a quiet-faced man who's been sharpening pencils, crumpling paper, twitching and mumbling a blue streak all afternoon. The shadow's cool shuts him up. During this moment of truce, as he traces circles in the dust on his desktop, curving endlessly around their empty centers, a certain image invariably springs to his mind. He's a little embarrassed. His thought's a cliché: white calendar pages that curl and are torn away in rapid succession by some indoor windstorm. This moment's hard on him. Fear of waiting, of the jailer's jingling keys, muted sounds growing louder, approaching down the long hall. Fear of the shadow that drives the light away. Ideas hurl themselves into his face like dirty words, and he'd like to lie down in some ritual position, facing east, to receive them. The phone rings. The interruption is brief. He returns to the picture he's trying to remember or visualize for the first time.

The setting is the great outdoors, amidst familiar rolling hills—actually bumps on the back of his father's head under his crew cut. The mood is a tense sobriety that tinkles like glass chimes in an evening breeze, giving its hiding-place away—a tender clarity, ever-fearful of backsliding into blind drunkenness again. He stares out the window. Eucalyptus leaves spiral onto the driveway. The time is back when he was poor and happier; before all his plans boomeranged. The conflict is that all the characters are trying to teach each other a well-deserved lesson. The theme is still up for grabs. But no one cares a fig for any of these dramatic elements, he thinks, except the setting. Pray it's exotic. *Transport us,* we plead, to where we ought to be. We want a rocky island—rocky but tropical, small enough to stroll around in half a day, before the tide comes in. We want pig sties, rows of hard dormitory beds with iron railings, bayous, seedy trailer parks, public aquariums, mine fields. Stuck in the geographical midst of the big picture that looms in his head when he sits down to write, he becomes dizzy, top-heavy, and needs a cigarette. He's a surveyor, who, after gazing about the landscape with a look of terror on his face, plunges his tripod into the earth, and shouts, "Here."

SAINTS

Miracle mongers. Bedwetters. Hair-shirted wonder workers. Shirkers of the soggy soggy earth. A bit touched, or wholly untouched living among us? They shrug their bodies off and waft with clouds of celestial perfume. No smooching for this crew, except for hems, and pictures of their mothers. . . their lips trespass only the very edges of succor. *Swarms of pious bees precede her.* One young girl wakes up with a ring on her finger and a hole in her throat. Another bled milk when her white thigh was punctured. All over the world, a few humans are born each decade with a great talent for suffering. They have gifts that enable them to sleep through their mistreatment: the sleep of the uncomplaining just, the sleep of the incomplete. Our relationship to them is the same as our relationship to trees: what they exhale, we breathe.

BZZZZZZZ

There's a certain beekeeper I've fallen in love with. His hair smells disheveled and fragrant as chaff. His bees are neither captives nor slaves. They're capricious. I'll follow their example. When he leads me into the cool green woods, I'll soothe and rule him. I'll open to reveal the complicated maze of my patiences, stored up since I was a tiny child. Beekeepers constitute a brotherhood. Their urine smells of pinenuts and justice. Each keeper is kept with his head in a cloud like a choirloft. Nectar-fed music is disclosed to him, coded in so many notes he feels handfuls of soot are being thrown in his face and he blinks like a simpleton. But soon the bees mold their keepers into sharp-eyed disciples. Honeybees swarm but cannot be sent out on missions. They dance and form first an anvil, then a breastplate of chain mail, then tornadoes and ancient sayings in the air. At last they serve as my wreath and veil. My love harvests their collective spirit made syrup. He bows to the murmured vernacular of pollen and wax. The sonata hovering over his head, that constant hum, is his promise to me: he'll bind us together with wild zigzag stitches and stings, since nothing but the bees can keep him.

*dancing around
the flush*

THE CURE

Just as the doctor promised, I've forgotten a lot. I barely remember that first place you sent me—those bald, dribbling women and nurses fat as tubas. Many x-rays later, I'm more of a glow than a real girl. A radiant skeleton in a billowing gown. Come take me home. This isn't my place, among odors of undone laundry and wrung hands. Well, it's September. They take us for long walks across the safe landscapes. They cut bouquets for our rooms. When you first arrive, they crop your hair short. Then the mountain air bites the back of your neck. The breathing machine makes a great deal of noise, but I can still sleep. I attend church services on Sunday. I'm not a believer but I love sitting among them. A sullen man to my right whose adam's apple jumps convulsively wants to share his bothersome thoughts with me. Better never to speak to anyone, to reseed this silence like the echo of lost talk caught in a dead woman's ear trumpet. He opens his palm and leans over to show me the little wrinkled map in his hand. His eyes gleam as if he's been eating uranium. There's no use explaining, crying, knitting or singing. Even this exquisite, vigorous prose you're reading right now isn't mine. It's his. I recognize the handwriting.

A LECTURE ON JEALOUSY

Jealousy can be smelled, if you've a nose for it, like mildew, garlic, or the fear-scented sweat rabid dogs find humans to bite by. Jealousy makes pastry taste bad, hobbles your gait, causes your right hand to write checks for sums your left hand never had. Jealousy can make sufferers hate harmless objects. Match-books, letters, eyebrow pencils—innocuous props we all need to fidget with, become EVIDENCE. The only known cure for this wasting disease is to cultivate a love for your rival. Earnest, passionate admiration, with all the tremblings and trimmings. Sleepless nights spent wondering "What does she have that I don't have/What does she leak that I've run dry of?" must be given over to serious research. Her white neck, her slender wrists, her great taste in A-line skirts, her confusion at stoplights, her old hands and young feet, her perfume—or is it coconut soap, the deft motion with which she flicks cigarette ashes hither and yon, her loud red blouse, her love of cherry tomatoes, her sneeze, her eggs benedict, her secrecy, the drone of her hair dryer, the amazing way she always looks like she's had her hair cut yesterday…see how easy it is? Her drug problem, her insomnia, her dress size, her polka-dot bikini, her pony skin wallet, her saliva which tastes so great…for god's sake, somebody stop me.

THE HOLY GHOST

lives in the clear liquid that flows through the veins of oak leaves. Whether that
fluid has been named or not. Known or unknown, visible or just guessed at, the
holy ghost is composed of what little light the prisoner sees through the weave of
her blindfold. The holy ghost is smoke and melodrama, the orange and pink
tongues of fire whiskey drinkers acquire when they hear the whiz of any
barmaid's whip, or their dead parents yelling at them. The holy ghost makes his
presence known the moment humans tune in to the everpresent din of all objects
talking at once: barstools squealing, the worried clink of glasses and sob and slop
of spirit—these sounds summon listeners, just as a mother catches her son's eye
and points to his pyjamas (like a fisherman beckoning with his net) to indicate
to the child he has stayed awake long past his bedtime. So it is that the holy
ghost holds his bullhorn, and his several voices ring in our ears worse than our
thundering drunken blood does. He orders us to hug everyone else in the bar,
saying "those who are by nature lovers are condemned to each other's arms."

[handwritten annotations: "biblical"; "essence of life"; ""he" makes the ghost human → holds, orders"; "First, meta, then rooted and grounded"]

WAR CRIMINAL

He wakes from another dream of his fascist youth, where he lay surrounded by the fruits of his skirmishes: a pile of broken bone china at his head, refugees' jewelry at his feet, heaps of fur coats and boots at his right and left hands. Women of all nationalities lolled nude on hammocks in the next room. But now his fatigue's currency is spent. He must wake, face the day, and relearn, as he does every morning, how all those he loved are now dead or elsewhere. Last night a train derailed. Search teams will probe the snow, and he'll join the rescue effort, wipe his brow at noon and glance heavenward. Even he can appreciate a flash of sunlight exposing two clouds' pink and silver collision, sans casualties. His eyes close. An animal pang: he hasn't eaten today, although there are plenty of crumbs in his pants pocket. He rubs his stubble chin, and opens his mouth, or something opens it for him and part of a phrase from an old folk song falls out. The song, grist from his conscience, betrays him. He's still gagging and wiping his lips when they lead him away.

THE UNFORESEEN

In Bible times heavenly messengers disguised as beggars were everywhere. Divine communiqués arrive nowadays via strange mediums. Meanings profuse and profound are inscribed in everyday life's most minor designs: the way glasses and plates rearranged themselves when our backs were turned, how my sisters and I seemed to read each other's minds, and times when something in the attic groaned at such appropriate moments. These were glimmers, little inklings, of what we longed for. At times, from our window, we'd watch homeless men skulk around our yard, exhibiting big discrepancies between their teeth. Father would send them away. But those poor prevented messengers! How could Father have known the effects his protections would have on four daughters, stuck in this small town few people ever leave? High hopes deteriorate here like houseboats sunk into mud at the bottom of an ancient Chinese waterway. We offer God strict, intimate prayers, but perhaps it would be better to simply admit our helplessness and send up waves of that agony instead. The homeless men paced under our windows at dusk, sometimes singing a little—"River Jordan is deep and wide / Milk and honey on the other side." Those lyrics, in earthy baritones, sung by shiftless sweating men, seemed to beckon us toward unchristian vistas. Something in the thirsty way they mouthed the word "milk" made me want to jump down from our window, into their midst, though it was some distance. These were sooty, threatening men, wearing huge weathered boots. Men with cabbage or worse on their breaths. Men on whom all clothing looked baggy and unnatural. Men who washed by sloshing trough-water on their chests and upper arms. We girls pined to be pinned down by something heavy and gruff. One of us would sometimes rub her cheek against a tree trunk, scraping her skin on its bark. There was one man in particular, less well built than the others. At noon I caught sight of him bending down, across the meadow. When he lifted his head, sunlight shone through his ears, giving them a red glow, and I remembered the blood in him. I could almost see his delicate, hairlike capillaries, and I thought about my downfall.

BITTER ANGEL

You appear in a tinny, nickel-and-dime light. The light of turned milk and gloved insults. It could be a gray light you're bathed in; at any rate, it isn't quite white. It's possible you show up coated with a finite layer of the dust that rubs off moths' wings onto kids' grubby fingers. Or you arrive cloaked in a toothache's smoldering glow. Or you stand wrapped like a maypole in rumpled streamers of light torn from threadbare bedsheets. Your gaze flickers like a silent film. You make me lose track. Which dim, deluded light did I last see you in? The light of extinction, most likely, where there are no more primitive tribesmen who worship clumps of human hair. No more roads that turn into snakes, or ribbons. There's no nightlife or lion's share, none of the black-and-red roulette wheels of methedrine that would-be seers like me dream of. You alone exist: eyes like locomotives. A terrible succession of images buffets you: human faces pile up in your sight, like heaps of some flunky's smudged, undone paperwork.

SLOW BOAT

This boat is slow, its bow glossing over Lake Como's breathless, echoed blue. Or the Dead Sea, or the Indian Ocean. Who knows? You choose. Where we are is all in our heads. Lie down now. No one wants to hurt you. Least of all me. I desire only the taut horizon, that famished threat of light. Right away. Remember when you almost drowned? Of course you don't. You've blotted it out. Hair plastered to your skull, you lay on the beach, sand stuck to your cheek, making one side of your face look unshaved. The shore rippled and tilted under our feet. Men moved their mouths but I lost the line of sound. Their faces ballooned, each a silent whirling, framed by an intense, wavy heat. There were black holes in the air, as if we were figures in a painting and someone had ripped the canvas in places to reveal gaping darknesses underneath. I never want to feel anything like that again.

Boy, this boat is so slow it seems to be traveling backwards. Flight into the past. A hurricane of girls begging "Let me play with your hair." But today, I'm more fascinated by your childhood than mine; the formation of your tastes. Does what I give up for you form an invisible heap at your feet? A pile of sacrifice you trip over in the kitchen? Sorry to leave it lying around. All I never said. Men never kissed to my heart's content. The word "listen" 's a contradiction when written on paper. My diction gets crisper when I tell lies. Your beauty makes me like a fossil sometimes. Encrusted, crumbling. I'm not fixated at any age…I don't have that much homeland or location. This vessel just drifts, I don't row. I'm a stowaway. I just roll in the dirt every day, disturb earthworms, fresh dead insects and live ones that need water to mate. What should I hold against you? Kissing her, then trying to push me downstairs, abetted by gin? What is it about your form, your dripping silhouette, I can't fully remember or forget, without a hypnotist's assistance? Drunk or heavy with love, I must think I'm your lifeguard. It's ridiculous…I can't swim. Last time I fell short. Not enough breath. I want to do it right this time. So won't have to do it again. My memory of your gestures can never hold a candle to the effect of your presence. How little Spain resembles its depiction on maps. The figurehead on this slow boat peers ahead into reefs and the gray mist of distant weather. She tests the current's temper, then it's past. I'm the foam on the waves, that licks her ever-parted lips. Only I know what she's floating toward or leaving behind.

RAY GONZALEZ

Ray Gonzalez is the author of *Memory Fever* (University of Arizona Press, 1999), a memoir, *Turtle Pictures* (Arizona, 2000), winner of the 2001 Minnesota Book Award for Poetry, and a collection of essays. *The Underground Heart: Essays From Hidden Landscapes* (Arizona, 2002). He is the author of eight books of poetry, including *The Hawk Temple at Tierra Grande* (BOA Editions, 2002) and *Human Crying Daisies: Prose Poems* (Red Hen Press, 2003). His two collections of short stories are *The Ghost of John Wayne* (Arizona, 2001), winner of a 2002 Western Heritage Award for Best Book of Short Fiction, and *Circling the Tortilla Dragon* (Creative Arts, 2002). His poetry has appeared in the 1999 and 2000 editions of *The Best American Poetry* (Scribners) and *The Pushcart Prize: Best of the Small Presses 2000* (Pushcart Press). He has served as Poetry Editor of The Bloomsbury Review for twenty-two years and founded LUNA, a poetry journal, in 1998. He is Full Professor of English at the University of Minnesota in Minneapolis.

A PAINTING IS NEVER IN LOVE

A painting is never in love with itself, its colors, nor the magnets hidden in its frame by the mad artist in search of fame. A painting is left on the wall for the quiet parade, the famous painter couple in the blue house hating each other for thirty years. Their paintings were never in love, the heart coming out of the heart trampled by uniformed masses lining up to be shot in the mural—their horrible expressions the look of angels who have learned too much, posed too often, familiar with the drunk artists' brushes covering what can never be regained. A painting is never in love with its criticism, avoiding the meaning the way the night thief dodges the devices, steals the masterpiece, and walks away. When he can't collect his millions, his treasure is buried in the first bombing, excavated twenty years later by a mistaken collector, his eye the only eye surviving the genocide to paint again. A painting is never in love with its history, the moment of creation returning to the artist in a vision of lilac gardens overrun by rings of shark teeth, the lone image never forgotten when the struggling painter wakes in the morning light and turns to the canvas illuminated by someone else's hands.

JOAN MIRO THREW A STONE AT GOD

God caught it and threw it back, forming two rivers, three continents, and supplying the painter with enough madness for five or six masterpieces. When I stepped in, I was drawn into the corner of the frame as a crack, a splinter down the side of the painting where my ideas became spider webs, the trail of paint drying into boulevards where I vanished one day, only to return as an impossible case, Miro sensing I was there but not saying a word as he climbed off his mistress, threw his brush aside, and buttoned his pants. God caught the brush and threw it back, the weight of the world varnishing Miro's failed canvas, streaking across his most sacred space where I tried to be the color blue, perhaps yellow, green squares where I breathed the moments Miro could never repossess, knots in his back forcing him to paint, covering me in black circles that began a period of suffering, Miro kneeling before me, brush in hand, his long hair of sweat demanding I return the color he wanted, the fumes of my possession burning in his chest.

HE CALLS HIS DOG RIMBAUD
after Charles Simic

The sausages have been sliced. The wine has grown old. The piano notes belong to the man lifting his hands from brushing Rimbaud, his dog. Women have left him. One or two poems belong in the books. He has a gift for knowing what people will do. He was cited as the one who found the image hidden inside the caves of the emperor. When he writes, his dog howls and gives him ideas to take on the boat. The hat and boots have been laid out. The perfumed photo of the woman has been torn. The piano notes settle in the soul of the quiet man hugging his pet and asking for a growl. He will meet the light on the next continent, walk toward it because everyone wants him to explain why other dogs ran away from him. He is driven to get to the source of this dog. He must find why the paws trouble his sleep, why he has to leave in order to speak and try to imitate the dumb dog by barking at nothing in the street. He must find why the wagging tongue of the animal hangs so far out of its mouth, so he calls out to his dog, "Rimbaud! Come here, boy!"

FUCKING AZTECS, PALOMAS, MEXICO

Small clay figures on a market shelf—eight couples entangled in different positions, Aztec men kneeling, mouths open, giving it from behind, one woman standing on her head, thighs spread as her mate sticks it in from above. The sculptor who molded the huge cocks laughs in an alley house somewhere in Palomas because the statues don't sell, turistas walking by the display without noticing because the Aztecs sit on the highest shelf, my curiosity spotting them by chance as I drew closer, stood on tiptoe, wondered what these tiny people were doing on top of each other, stone orgasm on their faces outlasting the dust collecting between their bodies. Looking closer, I saw their clay sex sweated in the heat of pyramids, legs and arms twisting around the god of the sun, a sacrifice of lust, distorted faces molded from the sculptor's hands, one set of figurines dancing a threesome—two women and one man the sandwich we have wanted our entire life, a taste of dirt from the shelf when I placed my fingers to my lips, stood back from the fucking Aztecs with their mud of passion surviving the conquest.

THE BLACK TORSO OF THE PHARAOH

He is extended singing. Let him in. Believe in his wish after his silence turns into scattered rugs on the floor of the mind. What? you ask. Where? How did his turtle make it to shore? When you raise your hands to feel for a pulse, do not hesitate. Plunge your arm all the way into the chest until you reach the greenhouse of the heart. When you pull out, say a prayer that doesn't lie, as something moves across the earth and he teaches you how to breathe. After all, the thunder you heard when you touched your belly button had nothing to do with the day you were born.

UNDERSTANDING

It appears as a woven fabric when you say something before anyone else. Voice and arrow take a different path to the same target. To suffer as if we have been taught well, we burn the image of the dead in the empty lot. They have no clue as to why you believe in those old piles of newspapers that appear as a woven fabric. The blossoming mimosa is a sign of things you can't find, your mind hungry, the tiny statue of an owl broken on the shelf. Speak without saying it and someone will listen. It is time to enter the waiting beehive without humming the same song, one thought underneath the striking moth, the flashing cat, the extreme arm of the squid frozen in ice, its slimy skin resembling a woven fabric. You will read this far without thinking a starfish glows. If there is no cathedral inside you, why are you so blind when the cripple removes his bandages one hour too soon, the light on his twisted arms writing on the intricate cloth for him?

AS IF TALKING

The necklace remains as the pet iguana lunges at the standing mirror when it sees itself. I was told to watch for the willow that resembles its tail, answer the face to see what it repeats of my beloved song. The fox crossed my path and looked back at me, its first appearance on my walk the last time I went that way—a pentagram handed off in the dark, on the pine cone a spot of blood, the frozen snail guiding the path. This world kissing the throne, someone wearing the beads, a voice nudging me awake. The old man moving his eyes in the painting, his chin getting warm without doves in flight. So the fox is red and disappears, burning permission granted. To touch its path with vowels. How strange to be seen under the cottonwood. This apple, the church without a forest, the wet night after I praise what I don't know, don't carry enough blame to silhouette my heart. In every broken necklace of love, the misspelled words.

THE BAT

The bat loved my belly button. It flew out of it when the caverns were no longer enough. Thousands of other bats ignored me, while my bat ate my thoughts and carried them south to the mountains where Cochise, the Apache, painted his face to resemble the flat-nosed rattler. My bat made it back into my hands that night, its beeping reminding me I left my jump rope in the shower, the sweat and pounds lifting higher than the line of bats encircling my car. When I went to bed that night, something motioned to me to start running because the bat that loved my belly button knew more about my body than I did. When the cloud of bats disappeared by morning, I found my lone bat crushed on the road, tire tracks lining its wings to resemble lifelines on the palms.

THE BLESSING

He survived the sacrifice and loved the world for not cutting out his tongue, leaving it intact in his mouth. When the invaders came, they left him alone because he was strange. They gave him glasses of milk and let him live in a purple house. He was angry about several things, but could not find the answers. He left an impression on those who spoke with him. He taught them about yellow colored birds, old tire rims, and the heavy earth. He composed songs to the wind and stood ready to pray every time it rained. When his father died, he moved out of the purple house and went to live with his mother. It was the wrong thing to do and he had trouble being remembered by anyone after that. It was not the kind of impression he wanted to leave because the momentous turn of the century was going to bring white crosses, family picnics, and secret places for him to put on his long white robe. He survived the sacrifice and loved the chance to be held in high esteem. When it was time for him to speak, people turned on their recording machines and let him listen to his voice, already captured when it ran across the air. It was the easiest thing to do for him. After all, he quit speaking five hundred years ago when the invaders left his tongue alone and gave him every chance in centuries to be heard.

TRADITIONAL

From the start, you won't disturb anything. They won't let you be the shuttered hand descending into the valley. From the beginning, you succumb to the pomegranate seeds on the cloth, identity of the approaching ship secure, the hymn dying on your tongue as you leave the room, go up against two men before they pull the hoods off their falcons, their wrists bloodied by a lie or two. From the middle, you memorize a captured document legendary in leading men astray, a folded napkin found in your coat when they cut your armor away, placed you at the head of the parade. You said it was manhood's thirst, soliloquy against damaged houses when you stood atop the wall, resembling a broken angel, a gargoyle from the comic books, your strange power they missed when you got tired and went to grow mushrooms in a valley known for its simple cures.

MAURICE
KILWEIN GUEVARA

Maurice Kilwein Guevara was born in 1961 in Belencito, Columbia and raised in Pittsburgh, Pennsylvania. He has received awards from the Bread Loaf Writers' Conference and the J. William Fulbright Commission. His books of poetry include *Postmortem* (University of Georgia Press, 1994), *Poems of the River Spirit* (University of Pittsburgh Press, 1996) and *Autobiography of So-and-so* (New Issues Press, 2001). He is a Professor of English at Indiana University of Pennsylvania.

READER OF THIS PAGE

I had a dream in my mother's womb three days before I was born.

I remember I was called Andrés Cuevas and I had a different mother whose eyes were lizardgreen and who lit candles and spoke softly of how cool the breeze would be in the new year. I had many fathers in the dream; each came into my world alone with long black hair, a harelip, and twelve fingers like me. Each taught me something of wood: One walked along the coast and pointed out to me the different groves of trees; one showed me how to shape branches with fire; one had precise knowledge of metals and whetstones, while another made tiny crosses with twigs and tied them in my hair. Time passed in the dream, and one by one my fathers died of lung soreness or jaundice or of staring at the face of God in the ocean. I built each his coffin and let him sail deep in the white hot sand. Then comes the part where I am burned alive on the second day of February, 1614.

I remember you, reader of this page, as I remember the soldiers in the dream leading us through the streets to the plaza of Cartagena de Indias—the carpenter, the sorcerer, the Portuguese, the Devil's gentleman, and the peddler. Screams, chants, official proclamations, music from a shawm: The Governor held high the banner of Santo Domingo and the <u>wooden cross</u> I made for you, a priest I have loved my whole life, <u>who read the final sentence, sweating.</u>

remembering
things that I can't
possibly be
remembered . . .

Dreamlike/
bending

MEMORIAL DAY

My father is singing in dialect over the grave of my great grandmother. The sun is setting. The country is in another war.

My mother is planting nasturtiums over Nonna's grave, her green skirt shorter than the grass. A northern shrike is piercing a songbird on a thorn of barbed wire. When the old veterans push the Catholic cemetery gates closed, brown bats start to ricochet in the violet-tangerine sky.

The twins' first memory is of silence and the slight trembling of semen.

⌈ BÚHO, BÚHO ⌉

Cuando sientas la barriga
como de puntillas llena
mascá raíz de manzanilla
con hojas de yerbabuena

—curación boyacense

We're stopped on the road from Belencito to Bogotá. In the convex sphere of an owl I see my six-month-old body cramping and weak in my mother's arms. My brothers are asleep next to us in the back seat. It's April, the rainy season. Many days and nights of diarrhea and wailing and vomiting and insomnia. Not able to drink even a coffeespoon of boiled water. The old doctor in our village finally showing the palms of his hands and turning his head to one side, as if to say: "Take this baby to the city before it's too late. My magic is from another time."

The old, borrowed Dodge has broken down in the middle of the mountain. My mother moves her wrist into the moonlight. 11:55. A small man and my father are under the hood with tools. My mother is quietly singing *"Reloj"* while holding the tip of her ring finger above my lips to feel the breathing. I see a match lighting a cigarette in the eye of the fluttering owl. The small man gets back in the driver's seat, looks over his shoulder at the lullaby, turns the key.

It begins to rain.

The last thing I see is my young father slamming the heavy hood.

NEW YEAR'S DAY

En el día más grande de mi vida, para los nenes la bendicion mia,
y que mis padres me den a mi bendición.

—R.C.

That night a particle of me rode a gigantic horse of coal, *Noche,* with great steel hooves that left a spray of green sparks falling into the Atlantic. Clemente's plane had gone down into the troubled waters beyond San Juan. For years I galloped along the shoreline in search of him. The fishermen said now he took many shapes: a sand shark, the evening tide, a taxi driver, a woman making *pasteles* in the market, a shirt on the back of a child, even Borinquen. But I don't believe in stories, so I ran *Noche* into the ocean and we explored the reefs and floor and found the bones of stingrays and brown rum bottles and collapsed fishing boats, but never the holy wreckage, fronds of his human body.

Never.

It took me almost ten years to believe this: Roberto Clemente was dead.

THE EXEGESIS

Plan Colombia funds the aerial spraying of coca and opium fields with Round up, the broad-spectrum herbicide patented by Monsanto…. (Agent Orange, interestingly, was also a Monsanto product.)
—George Monbiot

Washing clothes by the river, Luzmilda's eyes burn. Water. Washing. She beats the white blouse that balloons over the wide flat stone. GPS triangulates— electron data streams to the squadron of shining nozzles on each wing. They, like men, release. Ton by ton and time again, the buzzing blue sky atomizes. I think of ice crystals shimmering in the air over the Mon or Hue or Potomoc, a million knives rotating through space. Eyes contract. The child, waiting in the globe of water buried in Luzmilda, turns. Choking, she wrings the river water from the bloated cloth. And faraway the television tells us to beware of unmoored Saracens in crop dusters.

Ésta es una crónica de indias.

This plan fulfills the bestiary of olden times.

Witness the thick thighs of the prostrate Yolanda, sun bleeding from her to the Magdalena.

Witness Rodolfo born with no mouth.

None.

And this one is called Maria Teresa. Use that stethoscope to listen to the damaged rhythm of her heart.

The whine of the plane recedes beyond the scar of electric lines.

Luzmilda pins the sleeveless blouse that wants to fly.

In the tarpaper coop a cock with two beaks is pecking his way out of the dark shell.

AFTER MIDNIGHT AT THE SALVAGE YARD

How you leapt across the border of the high fence with barbed wire is still a mystery, miles and heaps of rusted steel and iron: beams, plates, axles, pipes large enough for grown men to pass through. The moon, a corroding disk, streaks down on a filthy miner, sitting, a masked coon at his feet.

His headlamp's a dim eye.

He looks at you, rubs the animal's back. "I'm sorry. Tell me if I told you before. Down at Graceton No. 5, ten minutes before the shift's up, timbers buckle, next second everything's black and here I am, or there. The woman in a white dress by the wrecking ball, with the yellow bird, do you see her yet? Sorry, that's just what I saw. Maybe you'll see something else." You turn, a doe jumping through you, seven arrows in her back.

AFTER CHAOS THEORY

This is the week before my mother's hysterectomy: she living with the word *cancer* inside of her, as the cocoon of fiber and blood remains inside of her, as I was once and have returned. Over my parents' house, a jet curves through darkness. Minutes pass. Then my mother says:

"On the radio they were talking about chaos theory, how the wingbeat of a butterfly on the coast of China, if nothing stopped it, could increase over time and space and completely destroy Los Angeles with wind."

FIRST APARTMENT

I move away from home to be alone.

The wood beside the keyhole is gouged and scarred. Some dark thing moves in my periphery. The interior is as cozy as a fibroid uterus: pigeon feathers outside the window and across the alley the manic pulse of a woofer. Ambulance sirens are chronic like this smell of curry and garlic and cat piss. I hear popping like popcorn coming from inside a twisted garbage bag left on the fire escape. I open my box of college books and lie down on the couch to read *Burmese Days*, smoking a joint after the first paragraph. A novel about freedom, I think, at which moment a glazed cockroach the color of coffee appears on my white T-shirt. Its antennae are alert like teenaged lovers. It hesitates before the text, curious: all those vatic words scrambling to escape, little Buddhas on the great delta.

SELF-PORTRAIT

It looks, at first, like a wall of blue sky, some cumulonimbus threatening to build up on the side by the fire exit. You need to walk to the other part of the canvas and get down on your knees and there I am by the floor: the size of a railroad spike. I'm naked, head shaved to the bone, and the bead of water that fell a minute ago from the ceiling magnifies by three times the point at which my feet are crossed. Only now is it possible to tell where the errant vein disappears into the ankle. The other sound, beside the tinnitus of air conditioning, is the unseen pounding from a forge.

A baby anaconda cords my neck like an emerald helix. These moth wings are spread like a dark bell in the city; my eyes are about to open. By chance, the long molecule of a pheromone has just caught on a lash.

RIVER SPIRITS

When animals were no longer people, I was walking with my young sons along the river of the sliding banks. Thick plugs of wild asparagus were pushing up through the earth, and in the darkness of the forest thousands of white flowers pricked our eyes like stars. My little one was kneeling in the mulch and pine brushes, pulling back the green vertebrae of a fern. Suddenly he called out. I thought perhaps he'd found fox scat or a white spider until we crouched beside him and saw the Monongahela village.

Dwellings stretched the length of a finger, wattled walls and matted roofs. Hunters in buckskin huddled around a stone, and we could smell the gray thread of burning tobacco. A line of waterfowl was flying north over the village, not far from the orange cooking fire. Under the widest part of the fern, the older children and five women were hunkering or bent in the garden, laughing and weeding around the goosefoot, the green pumpkins, the bright sunflowers taller than the old storytelling man drinking from a gourd.

"I am finished," he said, "it is the end."

JUAN FELIPE HERRERA

Poet and performance artist Juan Felipe Herrera is the author
of many books of poetry, prose, and books for children.
Among his collections of poetry are *Notebooks of a Chile
Verde Smuggler* (University of Arizona Press, 2002), *Giraffe on
Fire* (Arizona, 2001), *Border Crosser with a Lamborghini Dream*
(Arizona, 1999) and *Loteria Cards and Fortune Poems: A Book
of Lives* (City Lights Books, 1999). His memoir about his
travels in Chiapas, Mexico, *Mayan Drifter*, was published by
Temple University Press in 1997. He teaches literature and
writing at California State University in Fresno.

GIRAFFE ON FIRE

I sit on a gold vestibule. It isn't me.

This wavy swan to my naked left comes up to my bad eye. My dead eye. Catalonia, in its sacred and tiny voyage under the tectonic plates of Dali's edible sea. Swan's talons. Cobalt blue and geometric. Gold pearls and an inverted eggshell. My childhood, my little red daily missal, my edge of Plexiglas water. My breasts and my shoulders are sculpted and small. I raise my leg as I hold an invisible oblong figure in front of me. It is my gaze. Naked as Gala, Dali's lover. I know nothing. Nothing of Spain or its green-mantled skies. I live in a split sky. Yellowish without a sun, yet the sun envelops the firmament. The bottom is blue, then convex with a woman at the center. Mexico. Cortez. Malinche. East Los Angeles. San Francisco. El Paso, yes, the gate of all Mexican dreams—this soft animal, jagged with ragged dots behind its back that leads to a holy shrine. A wax cross always before me. I sit upright. Floating, my head tilted to the left. This is the proper stance in America, an adequate sexual crust that I eat as I ascend into the sky. It is not necessary to understand what is below me.

You must open your legs. You must figure the hard orange colors from your bill, then the black protrusion. This is innocence. I was born there. A fortune was discovered on my skin. My mother took me away one night. An egg was delivered, then tossed over a bridge. It cut into the waters, a shape of a man with tinted skin and a jelly heart. What could he do? He was alone inside the small canoe. What did he have? He had paints and a loaf of pumpernickel. He wanted to reach down into the water. The belly below him, floating up. Gala in white, in seaweed, in parables from Ezekiel and Port Ligat. Gala was elsewhere. Above him, as always. In front of him. As always. In a shrunken room dug into the bowels of a West Coast barrio. The barrio was insignificant. The fragrance was central to his existence. This is my language. There are no codes. She sits there. That is all. In eclipse. In fission. Hiroshima, Iraq. The San Joaquin Valley. In leather rubies and grape pesticides. Alive and willing, still. She is traveling sideways, onto Desolation and Desire. Avenues, voyages ripped from Cádiz and Cadáquez. Moors and Jews come to her.

This was my beginning. In the fields,
lost in the deserts of California. Many years ago.

AT THE EXODUS GYM/VALENCIA STREET

Jaime, lift weights. There is no suffering on earth, not even in rooms. You can feel onl
metal, white, pure, aluminum, the leather cushions, the hips churning against the be
structure, silver bricks pulling the legs forward cartilages, sinews; the gelatin dies. Th
arm in the center of the mat the arm, alone, hovering by the lights, the fist, the har
father's finger points Jaime. The virgin on your arm glows, the gold designs on her vei
flutter sweat, Jaime, there is no moon in this sky, no crescent of light underneath th
Adidas, only a horizon of mirrors, a band of loyal torsos burning fluorescent, curlin
into tight caskets of membrane, breathing out the voiceless kiss of pain, the handsom
smoke of soldiers training, counting the shifts of eyes, the enemies, practicing alie
maneuvers, silently, glaring, bending preparing for ambush, stalking in groups of thre
registering blood, going fast

to scream forever

in war. Jaime

Who are you? Bending at the jazz kitchen where they play Thelonius. Where they mash green doors on the piano keys. The pauses are significantly eternal. Police with crab suits. A Courbet above the door, framed in docile colors. Rag clouds in graffiti slime. Door is open.

This is all I have; an entrance to the kitchen, a fallow Stradivarius, wet with sputum and uterus. On top: the bridge puckers in Titian ochre. The torso, cut off. Lime water between the legs, tied and invented for the gaze jazz, the be-bop growl of someone standing like me. Congas, mambo skirts, a skull twisted into pleasure. This was our lot. At Tiananmen. Where we stood against the rectangles in green howl. This was our stance. Between a full line of Caruso and a wall of Auschwitz.

Build a guild, they told us. You must lay down the effigy. Gala must descend, she must be burned, they cried. But we held her up. In chalk dust. In a half-eaten dough ball, we carried her across the desert. This was our stance.I looked for Sarajevo and Kerouac. Velázquez had escaped. We stood there at the tables of the new inquisition. Our ceramic pottery still showed evidence of Moorish influence. They used our bowls to serve the soldiers clean water.

Arabs and Jews,
in broken Macehual Aztec.

We stood there with Gala above us. They turned their engines on and mutilated our widows. They turned the engines on and fed us rice gruel. This was our stance, in that significantly short afternoon by the kitchen's tawdry piano keys.

The Consulado stood their ground. They left us no choice. I looked for the Infanta. She was our last hope. Ruffled in sky throat. The music was at our left, it was inside one of the Friars' dining halls. Full of reddish cabinets, strewn hair and cut fingers. I stood alone in front of the mad cylinders, for a second. A little girl in Spanish muslin was sliding into the drilling groove. I wanted to reach out for her. I wanted to pluck another note from the vented and grilled steel.

Hold up the right corner of the sea, pleated. Lift it and find pleasure snoring, cut open by crystal and stone. Look down at your shadow by the sands, by the gilded whiteness of your legs.

Below you:

a wrapped hydrogen scarf, an ink cactus stuck to the dry galaxy below the sky veils. Touch down. Come to the ground, the talc, this desert—peeled and washed by distant clouds. My hair reddish, down to my jaws. When will I blow the conch shell? Shall I awaken the sleeper below? Who is he following with eyes closed? The perfume is solar. My nakedness is simplistic. As the sleeper searches, I find America rising on his back, mottled, brownish. Above the water, the stone folds, clutches itself, peeks through holes and rivets. We are playing. All of us, then just one. The sand has been swept with a wide brush. The girl—pensive as she lifts the folds of the water. One hand. One arm and on the other the conch shell waits. Poised.

I know the stone is the secret. The secret in the shut mouth. When I was five I cut my fingers. I cut off my thumb. I delivered ice on the back. Wolves sang from the mountains. Julián, the violin man next to us, in the Mexican village paced his floor. Julián knew his wife, Jesus, was shaking and another man was raising her hair.

LA LLORONA POWER-WOMAN CONFIDENTIAL

Classified Sheet: La Llorona Meets Dr. Espanto

Dess E. Torny-Yadda is one of her secret identities: a short, dark brunette with thick glasses, a mole on her left cheek and a knock-knee gait. Family from East Juárez, Chihuahua. Jumped the border illegally and took residence in El Paso, Texas. Graduated from Jefferson High and went on to UCLA; paid her way by selling Mayan herbal hang-over lotions to the Greek frats by Hedrick Hall.

Des E. is a human mask, a useful day to day moniker in the big city haze of mauve-colored offices, stiletto acquaintances, and smog squeezed personas. On a clear day you can flip your head back, gaze up and count most of the thirty-stories of the Barrel Linch TransAmerican Tower in the financial district of San Francisco. She now works as a broker on floor 27: International Investments. Her male Latino colleagues call her *desatornillada*, "screwy, crazy sell-out" or Dess for short. Envy, cold stares and menudo-smelling blazers do not phase DTY. Old macho dogs caught in a downward career spiral, these, she gobbles with a Granola bar and washes them down with a half cup of 2% fat milk as she downloads trade data from ITT and Microsoft.

"TY" is what her White co-workers call her when they see her stepping out to a Coho Salmon Cappuccino brunch with Dr. Espanto Esparza, the highest paid VP in the business.

"TY's got what it takes—brains, brains and more brains," they say biting their glossy fingernails, praying for a break.

What the junior brokers don't know is that by night TY takes on another ID. She presses the computer code at the gray marble entrance door in the private parking lot, slides up the elevator and swishes back into Espanto's terminal where she swims through the global files of Barrel Linch, milking accounts in Switzerland into guerrilla files in the Nicaraguan coast, undoing New York diamond notes and dropping them into the Underground Indian and Peasant Front on the border between Chiapas and Yucatán.

They call her "La Llorona" because, as the Indians say, "she has come back to save her children." In fact, "La Llorona" is her code name on the Internet; she appears and disappears in a key stroke. Bank of America, Banco Serfin, Banamex, Sumitomo, Maritime Arctic Bank of Commerce; they have all been gauged and bitten by the shadowy electric hand of "La Llorona." It is reported that Des E's current project is to hit W.H.A.T., otherwise known as W. Hey All Houser Timber Incorporated, in Seattle. A note was found in their quarterly Board of Directors agenda: "Eliminate environmental disaster, save the spotted owls and the last great Redwoods or I'll bite your heads off!"

Today Dr. Espanto, noticed that his Van Gogh Screen saver was jittery, the mouse pad upside down—there definitely was something wrong. His Virgen de Gaudalupe frame was turned backward. Espanto's family album of three. Shannon, his wife, Erin and Espantito, the cross-eyed baby was crooked as if someone had pulled the photos and then replaced them in a hurry. Breathing hard, he turned to get a cup of caffeine from his Espresso machine and saw the brief letter, a print-out, addressed to him:

Dr. Espanto:

"You've got exactly seven hours and seven minutes to change the fate of the world. And I am going to see that Destiny moves kindly. First of all, you must do the following (or boo-hoo: you may watch your family fotos on the next America's Most Wanted TV show, brought to you by the FBI computer files):

uno:

Deposit all the Washington DC. presidential lobby accounts into the #12Vata-Chiapas file;

dos:

Pentagon and NASA budget investments in earth movers, hydro-electric power loans and environmental clean-up accounts move to #441Chava-Rwanda account;

tres:

Promote all the women on your staff, immediately or I'll bite your head off!"
La Llorona

Dr. Espanto filled his Vesuvio cup with a double Expresso, sat down and stared into a Chinatown shrunken into a tiny green square down below. He took a bite from an old custard empanada pastry his mother had left him four months ago, on Father's Day. A funny taste radiated through his mouth, a musky air came up to his nostrils. As he crouched over his monitor and followed "La Llorona's" instructions, he sniffed again. The perfume was familiar. "Des E. Torny Yadda wears this kind of brand, 'Z-Lantro' — a fancy new rain forest musk made out of tropical grasses." Espanto whispered as he deleted the transactions. He would wait for the night; Dr. Espanto screwed his eyes. In a New-Age mask, one of those gray clear gels—with a red Bandanna and a black hat, he would peep behind his office door. Things were about to change fast. "Just wait, baby, " he laughed to himself with a new air of confidence, "tomorrow, in the Daily Salsa Examiner, in bold letters, the headline is gonna read: **Mystery Masked Man Saves Nation. Latina Culprit Captured by Exec!**"

To Be Continued...

"La Llorona's Last Tear
or
Will "Lowrider Sally Chingas" Rescue her old Sidekick from Jefferson High
and Save the Day?"

I, CITLALLI "LA LOCA" CIENFUEGOS: *SUTRA ON THE NOTEBOOK*

I stand alone, I hold a thousand lights in my teeth, my throat is sacred, my voice rises on its own, without the charter, only the rebel fuse, the wise elder mothers and my handsome lonely sharp faced teen sisters, we make a fire circle, we brew the necessary liquids and nectars, topaz, obsidian and emeraldine, reddish and deep, the cauldrons are full, who can decipher us, who can locate our braids, who can truly grasp our undulating hips and fill our hearts with black sweet light, the creation spurt, this song I am singing without names and numbers and myths of time and becoming, I ask you, leaning by the armored street future? Are you ready, are you willing, are you in position or will you walk on by and carry the notebook full of no thing you know or taste or die for? The machine waits for you too, the tubing, the ancestral mezzo mump transformer interpreter translator of your self in birth form. Hear it? Can you detect its sirens? Can you alter its passage through my city, this umbral specter of sleeping moth figures.

The little boy breathes inside the mother. You can see through him too. His blonde head turns below us. And the shadows of his legs stretch across the Great Waters of Ensenada where his sisters live. He has been blessed. No one can dispute this. The Consulado throw up their hands. They have left it all to Pedro Moya de Contreras. Yet, all is well with the child. Sarajevo favors him.

Anise, amaranth, and eucalyptus from Catalonia, in a vial around his neck; this protects him. He floats in his mother's invisible vestments. An absolute cipher hangs on a string and guides him through the journey to America. A conch of talc and divine powder, a pebbled pattern on the skin of sea creatures contains his future instructions. Today marks his arrival into the colony. The child belongs to the Ocelotl God.

The stones part over his mother's grave. The brain in the air, the one floating with cauliflower designs and a tiny red missal, with a parchment inscribed with his songs; they wait for him to lift his head, for his mother to open her hands and Siwanava to blow through his rectangular lungs. The child's name is Zapata.

EXILES

"and I heard an unending scream piercing nature."
—from the diary of Edvard Munch/1892

At the greyhound bus stations, at airports, at silent wharfs the bodies exit the crafts. Women, men, children; cast out from the new paradise.

They are not there in the homeland, in Argentina, not there in Santiago, Chile; never there no more in Montevideo, Uruguay and they are not here

in *America*

They are in exile: a slow scream across a yellow bridge the jaws stretched, widening, the eyes multiplied into blood orbits, torn, whirling, spilling between two slopes; the sea, black, swallowing all prayers, shadeless. Only tall faceless figures of pain flutter across the bridge. They pace in charred suits, the hands lift, point and ache and fly at sunset as cold dark birds. They will hover over the dead ones: a family shattered by military, buried by hunger, asleep now with the eyes burning echoes calling Joaquín, María, Andrea, Joaquín, Joaquín, Andrea,

en exilio

From here we see them, we the ones from here, not there or across, only here, without the bridge, without the arms as blue liquid quenching the secret thirst of unmarked graves, without our flesh journeying refuge or pilgrimage; not passengers on imaginary ships sailing between reef and sky, we that die here awake on Harrison Street, on Excelsior Avenue clutching the tenderness of chrome radios, whispering to the saints in supermarkets, motionless in the chasms of playgrounds, searching at 9 a.m. from our third floor cells, bowing mute, shoving the curtains with trembling speckled brown hands. Alone, we look out to the wires, the summer, to the newspapers wound in knots as matches for tenements. We that look out from our miniature vestibules, peering out from our old clothes, the father's well sewn plaid shirt pocket, an old woman's oversized wool sweater peering out from the make-shift kitchen. We peer out to the streets, to the parades, we the ones from here not there or across, from here, only here. Where is our exile? Who has taken it?

The gold triangle is my enemy.

It speaks with Chaucer's heart, rattles on about the English penchant for redemption, about the necessity for virgins in the time of holocaust. Calls me in a fake Pakistani accent, so I can take up my woman's vest and gather my sisters. 1 am coming from the left side, in my mother's white gauze, in my aunt's last handful of nickels. A circle of women climb above the mountain; Frida's again, Gertrude's, and Georgia's. The hand of a man wants to follow but he cannot. The Macehuales and the new Viceroy have sent the cadaver of Cortez back to Mexico City. In Seville, they grieve him, in Catalonia all is quiet, all is sacred. I am in love with Hera. I am reading the glyphs on her belly, tarnished coins with the face of Socrates. My thighs are muscular. Her skirt is shredded by my heat, by this ablution I make every Sunday morning. It is time to begin the inquisition, they are saying.

Behind me. The men are crawling and speaking in broken Aztec. They are saying the mulattos will win this war. They are afraid that the new God at the center will speak and stand on his mutton legs. Raise my cup and toast to Georgia. Raise my shadows. I walk on bone stilts to the mound where they dance. The earth is conical today. Angles and labia. Woven calf muscles. My head goes down. See that my womb is split and a red jacket reaches into me. Out of me. Bat wing. Testicles. Ovaries and cymbals in ash-colored clouds. Hide my face.

Take my eyes for nipples and suck. I want to carry this chair of hives and dancers. I want to solve these Spanish numbers. A brown blue, a gold fleshiness. Only the bust in the cave remains peaceful.

TAKING A BATH IN AZTLÁN

For Yermo & Susana Aranda.
Early San Diego Movimiento pioneers.1973.

For Rod Ricardo Livingstone

Fast for three days on arroz and sweet tortillas, water & prayers, round dance to copal, the incense that speaks into your ear, gives you inspiration, deep inside where there is light anise. Go to Yermo's at 4:00 am. He'll have the sweat-lodge ready in the back yard & the sacred stones will be filling themselves with yellow-red designs from grandfather fire, la luna will have blessed you already, just smell the night perfume—that's her, covering you with her silvery instructions. Go in now, now you are beginning, go in from the East asking for permission to be in the circle, you ask for it by the way you walk and move inside, it is all inside, the lodge, el fuego. Now, let the darkness speak to the left side of you, let the smoke of sage, giving steam-waves at the center surround you, point to you, coax your beauty, hoping for your tenderness to sing out, with your brothers & sisters, the ones you didn't know when you entered, listen to their sighs, they are your sighs in this one curled fragment, Little David prays out, a danzante, at the Centro cultural, a runaway, he is still searching, La Glory, who dances too, she speaks to herself, only Grandfather Fire can circle her words, whisper flickers, Yermo chants, eyes half-closed dreaming in, his shaky voices, pray out, he sings, your pain, burned, the one kept to yourself, suspended, call this out with green-deep breath into the fire stones, they are strong hearts, they will listen, take the raw pain from your shocked nest, upheld in the circle, give thanks, you are at the beginning, inside, empty, brilliant, leave your harsh skin, sweat, tears, still chirping below your belly, leave them open now where you kept them, at the center, lean with the cry, give thanks, the fragrance is thanking you too, walk out now, silvery again, blue-brown, out of the sacred womb-house, steam, water, earth, fire, this is what you are, coming, going, you join the earth, go up, then, to Yermo's after the sweat, in dance hunger, la cocina azul, get a bowl, hominy and menudo with blessings across the table, reach for the tortillas in a small basket of steam, in friendship, love, clarity & peace.

LOUIS JENKINS

Louis Jenkins' books of poetry include *An Almost Human Gesture* (Eighties Press and Ally Press, 1987), *All Tangled Up With the Living* (Nineties Press, 1991), *Nice Fish: New and Selected Prose Poems* (Holy Cow! Press, 1995) winner of the Minnesota Book Award, *Just Above Water* (Holy Cow! Press, 1997) and *The Winter Road* (Holy Cow! Press, 2000). He has read his poems on Prairie Home Companion and was a featured poet at the Geraldine R. Dodge Poetry Festival in 1996. His work appeared in *The Best American Poetry 1999* (Scribner). He lives in Duluth, Minnesota.

THE NAME

Instead of an idea a name comes to you, a name that no longer has any connection to the owner of the name. It comes as sound merely, rhythmic, musical, exotic and foreign to your ears, a sound full of distance and mystery. A name such as Desmond Tutu, Patrice Lamumba or Menachem Begin. You forget the names of acquaintances and the name of your first true love but this name comes to you. It repeats like a tune in your head. It refuses to go away, becomes a kind of mental mumbling. You say it to yourself over and over. It is your mantra, "Boutros Boutros Ghali…." Then suddenly as it came, the name vanishes.

Deep in the night, long after your own name has flown away, a voice wakes you from a sound sleep, a voice clear and certain as the voice that summoned Elijah, saying "Oksana Baiul."

LAUNDROMAT

Here you are again at the laundromat late Sunday evening. There are others here: the college student with his book, the woman in tight jeans, the mother with her noisy baby. It's not like the women gathered at the river, laughing and singing. This isn't a social occasion. Everyone seems bored, exhausted, anxious to finish the wash and go home. You're here now because of poor planning. This could have been done at a more congenial time. Well, how far ahead should one plan? Next week, next year, the next ice age...? Hard to believe but this is your real life, right now, watching the laundry go around. Something like watching television. And you are the star of the show, of course. Or maybe you aren't. Maybe you are only here as atmosphere, something peripheral, lending to a vague feeling of disappointment.

SOMERSAULT

Some children did handsprings or cartwheels. Those of us who were less athletically gifted did what we called somersaults, really a kind of forward roll. Head down in the summer grass, a push with the feet, then the world flipped upside-down and around. Your feet, which had been behind you, now stretched out in front. It was fun and we did it, laughing, again and again. Yet, as fun as it was, most of us, at some point, quit doing somersaults. But only recently, someone at Evening Rest (Managed Care for Seniors) discovered the potential value of somersaults as physical and emotional therapy for the aged, a recapturing of youth, perhaps. Every afternoon, weather permitting, the old people, despite their feeble protests, are led or wheeled onto the lawn, where each is personally and individually aided in the heels-over-head tumble into darkness. When the wind is right you can hear, even at this distance, the crying of those who have fallen and are unable to rise.

THE BEAR'S MONEY

Every fall before he goes to sleep a bear will put away five or six hundred dollars. Money he got from garbage cans, mostly. People throw away thousands of dollars every day, and around here a lot of it goes to bears. But what good is money to a bear? I mean, how many places are there that a bear can spend it? It's a good idea to first locate the bear's den, in fall after the leaves are down. Back on one of the old logging roads you'll find a tall pine or spruce covered with scratch marks, the bear runes, which translate to something like "Keep out. That means you!" You can rest assured that the bear and his money are nearby, in a cave or in a space dug out under some big tree roots. When you return in winter, a long hike on snowshoes, the bear will be sound asleep.... In a month or two he'll wake, groggy, out of sorts, ready to bite something, ready to rip something to shreds...but by then you'll be long gone, back in town, spending like a drunken sailor.

INSECTS

Insects never worry about where they are. A mosquito is so dedicated to the pursuit of warm blood that it neglects the long range plan. If a mosquito follows you into the house it waits patiently until the lights are out and you are nearly asleep then it heads straight for your ear. Suppose you miss, hit yourself in the head and knock yourself out and the mosquito succeeds in drawing blood. How will it get out of the house again to breed? What are its chances?

Insects don't seem to have a sense of place but require only a certain ambiance. A fly that gets driven 500 miles in a car and then is finally chased out the window does not miss the town where it spent its maggothood. Wherever this is it will be the same; a pile of dog shit, a tuna salad sandwich, a corpse.

WAR SURPLUS

Aisle after aisle of canvas and khaki, helmets and mess kits, duffel bags, pea coats, gas masks…. Somewhere there is a whole field of abandoned aircraft, all kinds, P-38's, B-25's…. All you have to do is wait until dark, climb over the fence, pull the blocks from the wheels, climb in, start the engines and taxi out to the strip. It's easy. You can fly without ever having had a lesson.

A beautiful woman dressed in black sits on a bench near a grave. A tall man in dress uniform stands beside her and puts his hand on her shoulder. She says, "I come here often, it is so peaceful." He says, "Before John died, he asked me to look after you." They embrace. Behind them are many neat rows of white crosses extending over a green hill where the flag is flying proudly.

The engines make a deep drone, a comforting sound, and the light from the instrument panel tells you everything is stable and right. Below are silver-tufted clouds and tiny enemy towns, lovely toy towns, all lighted by the bomber's moon.

THE UKRAINIAN EASTER EGG

It is quite different from the ordinary Ukrainian Easter Egg because of the pictures. On one side the sun is setting over Los Angeles and opposite, soldiers sitting in the muddy trenches. They look cold, smoking cigarettes. Here is the violin hidden in the soup kettle and there is a family of cats living in an abandoned gas station. There are so many pictures: the barbed wire and the road through the forest, the ducks, the radio, the yellow, smoky fires along the railroad track where the lovers are taking a walk. In the morning the elders of the village decide what must be done. A brave man must ride the fastest horse and deliver the egg. The journey is long, the roads are dangerous. The egg must be given only to the Czar.

VIOLENCE ON TELEVISION

It is best to turn on the set only after all the stations have gone off the air and just watch the snowfall. This is the other life you have been promising yourself; somewhere back in the woods, ten miles from the nearest town, and that just a wide place in the road with a tavern and a gas station. When you drive home, after midnight, half drunk, the roads are treacherous. And your wife is home alone, worried, looking anxiously out at the snow. This snow has been falling steadily for days, so steadily the snow plows can't keep up. So you drive slowly, peering down the road. And there! Did you see it? Just at the edge of your headlight beams, something, a large animal, or a man, crossed the road. Stop. There he is among the birches, a tall man wearing a white suit. No, it isn't a man. Whatever it is it motions to you, an almost human gesture, then retreats farther into the woods. He stops and motions again. The snow is piling up all around the car. Are you coming?

STONE ARCH, NATURAL ROCK FORMATION

It is higher, more narrow, more treacherous than we imagined. And here we are in a spot where there's no going back. It has become too dangerous to continue as we have. We simply are not as sure-footed and daring as we were when we started out. There's nothing to do but sit down, carefully, straddling the rock. Once seated I'm going to turn slightly and hand the bag of groceries back to you. Then I'm going to scoot ahead a few inches and turn again. If you then lean forward carefully and hand me the bag you will be able to move ahead to the spot I previously occupied. It is a miserably slow process and we still have the problem of the steep descent on the other side. But if we are patient, my love, I believe we will arrive safely on the ground again a few yards from where we began.

THE BOOK

Every night I read the same paragraph, the words of fire, the perfect symmetry! But it is impossible to hold. My eyes close and the book falls from my hands.... Sometime later in the night I wake, long enough to switch off the lamp and pull the blankets around me. By morning I've forgotten everything. Outside a gray workday drizzle is falling and the text is flat, uninspired. At night on the page between awake and asleep, the world makes perfect sense. There we meet again for the first time and you take my hand.

PETER JOHNSON

Peter Johnson's third book of prose poetry, *Miracles and Mortifications* (White Pine Press, 2001), received the 2001 James Laughlin Award of the Academy of American Poets. His other books of prose poetry are *Pretty Happy!* (White Pine, 1997) and *Love Poems for the Millennium* (Quale Press, 1998). His collection of short stories, *I'm a Man*, won Raincrow Press' 1997 Fiction Chapbook Contest. He is the founder and editor of *The Prose Poem: An International Journal*, and editor of *The Best of the Prose Poem: An International Journal* (White Pine Press, 2000). He teaches at Providence College in Providence, Rhode Island.

ENIGMA OF THE STIGMA, OR VICE VERSA
(for Genevieve)

I'm drawn to the ineffable, yet cathedrals leave me empty, the charismatic next door has no imagination, near misses of comets go unexplained by theories of emanation—all frauds, unsoiled neck braces piled in empty corners.

But I trust the stem of this feather, its eye a spot on the pillow where she lays her head, her rump warming the hollow of my stomach, lilies sprouting from a book on her nightstand, a perfumed hair creasing my tongue.... Mysteries inviting both penetration and erasure.

THE DOLL

Sits upright in an ancient chest, face smooth, expressionless as sanded bone. Could be anyone's doll. Not lazy, just sluggish from lack of visitors. No one to fix its damaged legs, pull the noose at its neck. No one to wipe beads of attic dust off its naked belly.

Imagine that belly, wave upon invisible wave of emptiness flooding its hollow. Imagine a ship of darkness exploring plastic channels in its chest, arms, head.

A toddler discovers it, fingers sticky with ice cream, a face fleshy and pink with delight. She lifts it overhead with inexperienced hands, lets it fall, picks it up again, strong-arms it to her chest. "Love, love," she says, dirtying her white dress. "Love, love," she says, dropping the doll onto the floor, kneading the air with crooked fingers, smiling like a toothless angel who doesn't know better.

DARWIN

Charles, we collect beetles too, red ants, horseflies, even tomato worms. But I like my bees in a bottle, my bulbs basketed. And why are we here, my beamish boy? "The sight of a naked savage in his native land is an event which can never be forgotten." Charles wrote that by lamplight as he watched fireflies jitterbug on the horizon. He saw God in a sea hedgehog, in an orchid, then a theory appeared, sudden and frightening as a new planet. It must have been difficult to kill God, like hugging a porcupine, like being bitten on the tongue by a dung beetle. "I am not an animal, I am a plant," you laugh—a remark dumb enough to renew my interest in self-fertilization...We're docked off the cliffs of Patagonia, fighting over the name of our new lovebird. You want to call him "Tupac," I like *"Dasein."* Charles has no idea what we're talking about. Later, he's climbing a chaos of rocks, extracting bits of seashells from a cliff. Sea creatures in the mountains? How did it all start? "Perhaps a great egg came forth," you offer, peeling off your "Gotta Sweat!" T-shirt. I say to picture God as a tone-deaf, handsome accordion player clinging hopelessly to his failed lounge act. And your cruel response? "Another useless metaphor from the Incredible Shrinking Penis." Which makes Charles laugh, no doubt thinking he'd like to see such a phenomenon, perhaps probe it with a sharp needle.

THE NEW COUNTRY

I was with my grandfather when the boat landed. He said he was a policeman, a crook, or maybe a priest. He smelled terrible, and you could see the Old Sod caked under his fingernails. He kissed the ground and headed west, knowing little except that he'd resent his offspring. He wasn't married then. I, just a glimmer of a glimmer in his bloodshot eye.

GUY TALK

My son asks, "What does it mean when you're watching TV and your dick gets hard?" "Change the channel," I say, "and when you speak to me, call your dick a penis." Though I never did. We had more names for our penises than the Greeks had for gods: pecker, dink, swanzola.... You've heard them, seen the boys laughing behind the sand dunes lost in their fathers' dirty magazines. What fascination! How they simultaneously run and grip themselves while filling the air with soccer balls. How, as adults, these same boys display and measure their members on a specially designed cutting board, so that afterwards, a pecker order decided, they can speak honestly with each other. If just for a moment.

PROVINCETOWN

We laughed about the pine tree laying its eggs, the blue fright wig I bought last Halloween, then a little wine, and a little more. The bed next door began creaking a foreign, same-sex language. I was reading a thin book wherein a fat lady wrestles with nouns. A book taking sixty years to flower. Later, we stumbled into a tree-shaded courtyard where white marble lions drank from an albatross' basin. We had run out of booze, and I kept having to pee. "So go one last time," and "Okay, I will." The mean mosaic of the courtyard floor was making me dizzy, anyway. Off-season, the narrow streets were barren, the frigid, salt air from another century when wreckers scoured the beaches for boxes and barrels. "Gigi," I said, "in the fall the cows here often feed on cods' heads! Did you know that?" "And capybaras have webbed feet and are excellent swimmers," she replied, understanding my foreplay. We would have continued if not for a large poster of a petrified, Amazonian face eyeballing us from a tarred telephone pole. "The Fat Bitch Is Back," the poster announced. And we had to believe it, suddenly confronted by a woman dressed like a bird cage, and another like an umbrella. Really nice people, though, in spite of their cheap costumes. "Are we hungry yet? Are we downright famished?" Gigi nodded, knowing a loss is not a great loss, and that the liquor stores didn't close until midnight.

NEANDERTHAL

A head-shaped cloud takes a bite out of this prehistoric sun. We're staring at the silent pubic bone of a long-dead ancestor, a spear sticking out of his fractured skull. If you just had more facial hair we wouldn't be so conspicuous. And those perfect teeth are bound to piss them off. I remember this: "Some Neanderthals would suck brains from the skulls of their enemies." So tread lightly, my boy, blend in. We'll dust ourselves with clay and fossilized feces, fashion a tool driven by a concept, something to blow their little minds. They'll think we're gods with our little heads and big ideas. Or maybe we'll interbreed, give future bone-diggers something to ponder.... Nearby, the sound of pee spraying the outside wall of our tiny cave. Peer over a boulder, and there he is: *Homo sapiens neanderthalensis*— squat and hairy-shouldered, with the exaggerated calves and biceps of a sumo wrestler, and a rocking gait, as if he just gave birth to a boulder. Ain't no pebble chopper, this one—instead, our future and our doom. So let's join the clan, spend days driving hyenas out of caves, nights waving lit branches overhead, dancing, as saggy-breasted females scratch out images of animals on a limestone wall. And our mission? To make everything noteworthy, of course—even this bear claw, even this pile of dung...

HOME

If there is no Gigi, there is still her name…To be sure, a long winter, but now a spring breeze, like a sigh, carries us to the edge of our sheets. Across the hall, a tow-headed boy moans, tumbling from one clumsy dream to another. Adolescence—rascality, pure rascality! Tempestuated, like the crocuses gazing up in a panic, all too aware of their short-term erections. They know a Big Idea is ajar, our trip tripped. It was all too exhausting, anyway—the hotels, the intrigues. Better to hunker down, mine the backyard mulch for anemic worms, go fishing. Or maybe lie still a moment, contemplate the scars on your feet, the ant-sized beauty mark on your bum. The mailman sighs when you open the front door in a silk kimono. I sigh when you open any door. I swear this before our sharp-beaked lovebirds just now awakening in their golden cage, exchanging necklaces crafted from the legs of a spider; before the sacred shield of Jean de Jean, hanging in our garage next to the bicycle rack; before my yang, growing warm, hard, steadfast. "See?" you laugh. "This is how you get into trouble." And, of course, you're right. But I fear our fairy tale is fading—friends coupling and uncoupling in various unseemly ways. So again I plead, "Speak louder to me, mother dear. A bit of pancake, please, I am so hungry," and you pat me on the head and reply, "Oh, darling, pretty, good, nice, clever, sweet darling…."

NETTLES

"She was running in the field with the tall nettles," but there were no nettles in my neighborhood. Just a line I stole. But she was running in the field. There was a fight. I looked on in tranquil wonder. Chains, like bats, flying from black leather jackets. She was yelling, "Get help," knives swaying back and forth in the tall field. I yanked on my scapular. She was running because it was over her, because of things she did I could only imagine. She was running, barefoot and bruised in the tall field. She had never heard the word "nettles." Even I wouldn't come upon it until years later.

RETURN

End of the twentieth century and I'm still angry. The new hero same as the old hero. And the poets? They're out back wrestling in the wet mulch, writing each other love letters with bird shit on brown paper bags. Just want to don my pajamas and curl up with a good book, but there aren't any. "Take it easy, Lady Philosophy," you warn. "Whoa there, Mr. Negativity." You're pointing to your souvenirs: jodhpurs from Jodhpur, an artificial ass from the court of Louis XIV, an eyelash of Catherine the Great. I shave my head, put on my swim cap limed with Bengay. I sit in a corner, sifting through the ashes of famous people. It's a metaphor, gentle reader. It's not a metaphor, gentle reader. Like everyone else, we wanted to become a legend, or a footnote to an obscure anecdote. We were driven by the certainty of heavy soil and that starlet's buttocks. And I wanted to Educate you, and would have, if the cockroaches hadn't eaten our canoe. There was certainly no ostriching on my part; I faced down every truth, every falsehood. "On my trip I met a woman named DNA," you croon, with that silly look on your face, then ask to play outside with the Famous Poet, who's holding a sacred fish over his head, saying, "When the hook is caught in the lower jaw that means your *vahine* has been unfaithful." This is not a metaphor, gentle reader. Not even a Strange Fact of the Week. Just a little jab to keep us moving, to keep us on the run.

GEORGE KALAMARAS

George Kalamaras's poems and prose poems have appeared in *Best American Poetry 1997, Luna, The Prose Poem, Sulfur, TriQuarterly,* and elsewhere. He is the author of *The Theory and Function of Mangoes* (Four Way Books, 2000), which won the Four Way Books Intro Series Award, and two poetry chapbooks, *Heart Without End* (Leaping Mountain Press, 1986) and *Beneath the Breath* (Tilton House, 1988). Among his awards are a 1993 NEA Poetry Fellowship and the *Abiko Quarterly* (Japan) Poetry Award. He is Associate Professor of English at Indiana University-Purdue University Fort Wayne.

THE SENTENCE
for the poet, _____*

He lives, he said, for the pure joy of a sentence, for the slantwise grip slicing back through the clock. Scissors hands laid out on the table resemble a ballerina exhausted from the weight yet still pointing one foot forward toward the food that could be and one backward toward a thinning wire that passed through her cells and shaped her. *Poets belong to a cult of the Word,* he said, carving his name in seven languages over and over in secret into his chest. He knew the letters by heart. He knew the chest hair would be years in growing back. He knew his hand would sweat and tremble whenever he smelled lead and heard the dog pant and express its stool. He knew the heart would be near and far. He knew he had blood on his hands. A Chinese junk slowly crept by from out of the bathroom mirror into a burlap cloud, then into the mouth of a frog, as if no longer needing water. The sail-crumple, what he felt every time he collapsed a word and unhurled it from his chest. *I keep thinking that if I could write, I'd write not a Bible, not the Psalms, not the Koran or some Upanishad, not even warm peony blossoms of T'ang Dynasty love, nor the pumping forth of bleached blood-angels before me on the table in piles of speckled sea salt, or weeks of split shifts without sleep, or thin shaved legs afterward in the clutching in the dark, or newly fallen snow without the salt or the seed, without spleen or wing.* A quonset hut glowed in the snow-covered night, and so much substance piled around it at the roadside as if he might learn not to swerve, as if camping at midnight in the echoing slush of passing trucks might relocate a gravelly period between letters and not sentences, words. *We write,* he whispered into the bathroom mirror, *toward the extinction of the personality.* He wanted to write not a Bible, nor the Psalms, nor some undiscovered Upanishad, nor even a controversial verse for the Koran. He wanted breasts and he wanted milk. He wanted the red red snow of peony blossoms. And he wanted them now. He wanted the night-glow of the quonset hut as sun in his groin. He wanted a scrotum without motion, without pearls, though the pearls could come, he conceded, if that was the only way to finally find flight.

*Reader Insert one of the following:
a. name of poet believed to be subject
b. name of author of this prose poem
c. if different, name of both believed subject and
believed author (otherwise repeat name)

d. reader's own name (if female, change pronouns and
anatomical references accordingly)
e. name of favorite inanimate object with poetic
propensity
f. none of the above

A PROCLITIC STITCH IN THE VERTICAL PULL OF ROBERTO JUARROZ

It is written somewhere—either in a book or a tree's wind—that *The way up and the way down are the same.* Some say, *Heraclitus,* while looking in the mirror, bloated with morning breath and eye resin. Others repeat, *A wound in my abdomen.* Others, *And if I would only have eaten less salt!* Still others say, simply, *Juarroz. Roberto Juarroz.*

It is inscribed that it is difficult to decide where, exactly, it is inscribed. It is also written (though rumored thus), *Try it yourself and see.* If you find this phrase, can indeed read and decipher it, you'll soon see that you are blind as a person regaining sound, temporarily. The letters may blur, your speech slur, and what allows your lips certainly not a word. It is written, either in the long hair of the willow or in the thin fire of the Chinese Elm, that, *I found a man writing on his bones.* While some whisper, *Sad sad elephant tusk in the heart,* others are certain that Roberto Juarroz dies and ascends every morning in the crust of each eye. At least, that's what the mirror suggests to each eye, independently, mountain back of a nose keeping one cavern from the other, crust in the corner, a moss of clear altitudinal water. And thus, Juarroz is rumored to see the world anew each morning through the multiple bones of so many faces awakening for the first time unto themselves.

Somewhere—anywhere—either in book, bone, or tree, there is absolutely nothing written. No writing except for merely the sound, *No writing.* No sound, even, except for that sadness stitched in the chest (but sewn not as music or vowel and, certainly, not in the heart). Either vertically or horizontally, it is difficult to discern, though it's the stitch and not the direction of the incision that resonates. Impersonal. Abstract. Discursive. Void of history and context. Aphoristic. Stitch resembling tracks of a faraway train in the lush Argentinian pampa surrounding the little town, Coronel Dorrego, in which, in 1925, the poet Juarroz was born. Or, perhaps, more vague, inexact, like—simply—the disappearance of the words *town* or *grass.* Or perhaps even as remote as *a mode of transport in the 20's between distant cities, no, between distant* **destinations**. Or resembling just simply the absence of the word, *birth,* as it has been proven that each person is indeed *born* (though what that constitutes, linguistically, is subject to debate).

Still, the paradox, some say, is introduced into everyone at birth, inserted as the sound, *Heraclitus,* into the gum preceding tooth, and surfacing—years hence—as a stutter in the syllables *Juarroz,* which one comes upon quite suddenly one morning after an evening of salt. A stutter, even, in the vowels of *Roberto,* which bloats the mirror with morning breath or scabs it with eye resin. It is almost written, then, that the paradox may in fact be a wound, or the wound a world. But most certainly, it is known (at least by the hum of a very silent sound) that the paradox persists, that—in at least three of two directions—the way up continuously sinks into the stitch in the chest (train on the track or absent, horizontal verity or vertical horizon) as it tries to climb, this climb, this endless falling forth.

TO LIVE IN PRONOUNS: THE BIRTH OF PEDRO SALINAS

He lived his life inside a pronoun. His entire Pedro, his Salinas. Such a sad world before the evening thunder of 1892. Before the birth-bag burst and dropped net of starlight. Before the goldfish fin scattered tiny eggs in sand. Before each egg, a sag. Before each hatch of moon.

Plum gold, they say. With their entire, with their protruded paradoxical yet puckered. With their belief in the redemptive sway of a suspension bridge. As some tell it color at that time was not yet sound. Mouths, not nearly vowel. Even the jungles of Peru opened an ocean away to receive, as their own, part of his birth. The world prior to his Salinas, to even his Pedro, could have, should have been called, *already spoken,* or *banished from the forest,* or *ask your mouse blood while touching the owl's terrible rib.*

Resinous mouth of a mother, biting down hard on a pine cone, screaming her sweat-drenched body, her entire Salinas self, her prior pubescent Leon, maiden name moan, into the midwife's olive oil salve across her crotch. Starlight on each salt bead against the wall, a candle gaining itself to ash, *Senora, Senora Salinas. Call him pine resin. Call him tyto alba. Call him Him.*

Too many names. Nouns. Barn owls. So she, they, from the bottom of their Salinas from deep within her Leon, settled on *Him.* Not Pedro Salinas as wet. Not the dark fill in the county court. In the still drying. In the large case. In the corridor and its immense imitation of the cord. But in the inky net, the nest criss-crossing its twig Journey between worlds. Words. Terrible ribs buttressing all they could suspend Could eat, even, from the weakest worm of a limb.

Such a sad thunder before the wells. Of 1892. Of the moon and its dew. Before the goldfish finch and lowering of the bucket. Before the tiny. Before the scattered Before dust from his Pedro, from his not-yet-solidified-Salinas bone. Milk moiling from the breast of his mother, from all her years of dolls and tea cups and being tucked in as a Leon. Sag of egg in the sag of misplaced moon. Twenty-eight days in the stay. Sky turning the continuous worm of chert with, *Pedro, my baby.* With *Salinas, my most moist youth.* Crouch of noun in the pronoun's pouch of shame mouthing. *Hey You! Him! It!*

THE DEATH OF ATTILA JOZSEF

Attila Jozsef didn't die of fright, as they say. No, he loved the black soil too much and became all that he loved. Someone said it was suicide, the sudden, prolonged starlight of a bullet, canyon drop of a hunting knife hidden in a left sock. Someone else said it was an accident, like that of the Greek romantic poet Angelos Sikelianos who drank, at his bedside, that glass of lye he thought was medicine the nurse had laid out for a cold. Or like the onion skin lungs and sheepherder's hair of Miguel Hernandez, mistaken in Franco's prison as a way out, a midnight Silk Road route for the rats. Jozsef, they say, overdosed on ink, the underwater murk of some deranged squid, intentionally put the quill on the verandah until some great angry bird swooped down and scooped out his eyes, looking for worms. But Attila Jozsef didn't die of fright. He went down to the winter river, Fekete, searching for salt. Got down on all fours and knelled like a wild Hungarian pony, kneeling on its mournful hocks, exiled from the sweet dark grass of Black Forest spring. Rolled his massive broad back over to scratch out the bites of flies, and saw the dim rich soil depth, he so loved, above him in a starless night. *Oh, the Black Forest, the lovely Black Forest, is up there too, is all around—even here in Magyarorszag!*, he moaned with something like a wagon load in his voice. *And the inky black ice floes of the river Fekete must certainly be the blackthorn sap of winter sloe, the gestating haystacks and lush ribgrass of Ijssel Glen, broken ponds of Black Forest sky!* He looked to his left and saw the river's edge as a slice of Hungarian dark rye. No, Attila Jozsef didn't die of hunger, didn't die of fright. He loved the black soil too much to ever leave it, alone.

LEMON SEEDS OF YANNIS RITSOS

So you've heard that Yannis Ritsos used to sleep with tiny lemon wedges between his toes? That he'd roam the evening streets of Athens for the proper color—not quite wild thrush yellow, not really marble green, never Metaxa brown? That he'd barter a leaflet of lamp-lit written Socialist poems to have his paring knife sharpened just so, but always of delicate pulse on the blacksmith's stone? A sparrow might appear from flint chips, lift an instant and become moon? Hay in the corner would curve into the proud, pleading shape of a sickle? The blacksmith would begin feeding the leaflet, page by yellowed page, to the one old mare curiously nuzzling Yannis's lemon-scented pockets?

So you say you've seen Yannis through the tiny apartment window return and pull, first, each acidic seed from his pockets, then the lemons, one by one, still whole yet somehow seedless? That the paring knife remained in a pen case on his desk beneath the lantern? That sparrows suddenly appeared outside in the geranium window pots like drops of anvil moon, flew through the jagged lightning crack across the pane, and became moths? That the linseed oil of the lantern flashed with the beating of wings and green velvet? And there was light?

You don't believe any of it, you say? Have never believed your own people could bleed, that Yannis's tuberculosis could have been barbed into him by wire seeds? The kicks in the head and gut by officially approved Junta fruit? Scars on his hands by jutted glasses of juice in which, imprisoned on Macronisos, he buried his poems to secure them from the guards? Yet now you also *don't* believe that you don't believe? It was the seeds, you say? The invisible fence within the pale plasma of a deranged geranium, choking out the light, even if it was only moon-glow? Your struggle to see them, abandoned, through strangling red leaves? The way the seeds seemed to seep pools of polished glass onto the mahogany table when he took up a pen and began to cut the rind and juicy pulp without them? First one lemon, then the next? Slice after slice? Then the door crack and pale glow and the tender bending after his bath, towel-slip to his knees, like a woman painting her toes? Wedge by saffron wedge? Eight seedless sickle moons? Eight moist edges, like the down of damp cotton balls between toes, that no longer touched? And afterwards, Yannis pausing on the stool, cigarette between two fingers skin-shriveled from steam? Deep drags of after-bath smoke sinking and caressing his toes?

So you say you've heard and seen? That you believe and don't believe? That, unexplainably, the oil lamp on the table still smokes velvet green? That, though he's dead now, you're certain—or nearly certain—of the table stains, the ring of salt, the almost ovular wailing, the seeds?

LUCIEN BLAGA WAS NOT A FISH

No, not a carp in the bottom of some Hindu temple pool. Nor shad suddenly at the foot of the bed like an unwanted whiskey fifth. Transylvania heat, they said. That's how birds happen to flight. Rain on the tin-roofed shed near Rupen. Something that stinks and stinks and stinks. Whether the Rhine becomes the Waal or the Ijssel never mattered much to hay. Lucien Blaga knew that like he knew salmon rush in totem spring among tribes of the American Northwest. Though he never left Europe, he trusted that he must. Could have. Should have. And probably did. In some previous incarnation, Cantonese lilacs had been blackthorn blossoming plum outside Carpathian snow-melt. Where might a ripe black bat wing a world alive? Bee hives in Lucien's throat. In the gypsy stake mistakenly plunged in his heart. By his own hand, he lost the bet that one glass of draught equaled two black bass thumping the sand. The bed. Oh God, what did the feet feel as thrust down there that hushed? Every manner of voice in Transylvanian night was myth. That's what woods were made of. The corduroy bark. An ascot like a silk hand folded at the throat. That's what Lucien spoke— moth capes, fishscapes, starlit hay shapes—like pure, Carpathian gill-fire startling the wild ponies, drawing snow up from river-sunk moons as though from a grassy fin-flash well. Not a carp, no. Not a conductor's baton tossed to rust in a Banaras temple pool (that was music not flung moist enough east). Lucien Blaga was not a fish, not a fifth, not the cylinder scraping into shape silver-bullet Transylvanian dew. Though what he spoke cast moon bubbles as honey-comb lungs below lice floes and showed how the world could stink and stink and stink.

BLAS DE OTERO AND THE PANTRY OF BLOOD

"The kitchen is the most surrealist thing in the house." —Blas de Otero

The pantry asked for something more. Aprons, oranges, blood. The kitchen dirt of Blas de Otero and a Howitzer stove firmed in 1937. Its door opened and shut, the way an eyelid craves death—that's all he knew. For a very long time peasants from Viet Nam inhabited the pantry, until one day when there was no more rice. For a long drink, the Arabian horse betrayed its owner and, kicking over a shelf, looked almost content. For many turns the Madrid theatre gate (imported as a decorative accessory) kept reflecting smudges of so many confused hips having asked themselves in their grindings. *Which is more surreal—a kitchen, a pantry, or a film?* The pantry asked for something—anything—more. For Blas de Otero to leave the kitchen, return to Spain. For the film of the Republic to rewind itself and salve the eyes. For Blas de Otero to abandon the caves in Cuba. Asparagus in Indo-Chine. To once again pick up that pencil nub and thrust it into the neck of all those back home whom he loved, or would ever hope to love.

Aprons, dust, coal-colored juice, Havana cigars. Even in Cuba, while he had been out, someone had been sleeping in his bed, listening to music with his fork, had even eaten asparagus stored in cans—though he had been gone only an hour, he could smell its sulfur already in the next room in the toilet. The pantry door opened and closed, like a fist full of coffee-beans. Like a threatening in the heart trembling to choke the wrist. Like the eyes of Blas de Otero as he pinned the napkin to the neck and tenderly, almost cruelly, fed spoonfuls of Franco to Franco himself, over and over again.

BELGISCH CONGO, CONGO BELGE

It's been thirty-six years since I sailed the River Congo, northeast to a village in search of Kinshasha. It had all been simple pubescent pain. Hunched in a room thirty feet from the divorce, I poured over squares and rectangles of inky blue, slate, carmine, olive gray, listening to the bend of grass huts across river from the French in Brazzaville, hearing my mother and new father argue over drumming and dancing and pounding falls about the cost of lawn furniture, the merits of cold mashed potatoes, the young blonde flirt with long legs in the Wednesday night bowling league in Lowell. All that unresolved doubt she must have felt, and me, clinging to tall men haloed in ostrich feathers who pressed spears into the African veldt like fierce spines that stood me right in bamboo groves far from Indiana, where I was certain my light was destined to be darkly lit.

My father never phoned again when I slipped that first September and called my new dad, *Dad.* Nine years old was too young for a life sentence, I knew, though I had my own room, and black and white t.v., and got A's in Phonics and English and Math. Full-bellied zebras, round-rumped okapi, and undressed breasts fed into me from below. All I knew was that the stirring in my groin was the pound of pouring water I longed to touch, and in touching clutched the desire for more. *New wallpaper,* my mother said, and the hall blossomed velvet roses raised slightly like gooseflesh a mid-August wind might suddenly bring in reminding you of books and bells. *Shag carpeting,* she spoke, and the den was drenched in orange and rust. Even the plastic rake hid in the closet, fearing the bend. As if reaching down that far might be enough to strain the prongs and make it break. *An artificial palm,* she stroked the brush of his 5 o'clock shadow, and the living room was almost alive.

Beyond the Port of Matadi, all the way passed Leopoldville, hunched within the parameters of a perfect perforation of 13, was Inkissi Falls. I knew every hang of those falls, every leathery boa river bend, the River Ritshuru, the River Molindi, the Suza, even east of them, by land, through the bush and plane trees of Mitumba across the border to Ruanda and Urundi—occupied German East Africa. Spoils of war. I knew the bottom dropped out for a purpose. I knew the man with the wooden spear would splinter bamboo forests in rain and fight the Belgians and save the village from malaria, missions, sleeping sickness, and flies. Huts wretched in the wet. The smell of straw mixed with cow urine and dung. The salt and juice of life that shot out warm and thick and sticky and further than the Belgian nuns might go, or could go, that lent more, even, to the land than the argument over Christ or Thunder, Flemish or French.

More potatoes, my new dad would say, and the plates were filled with blots of boiled light. *More pot roast,* he'd request, and mother would brush the bend of red hair from her face and smile over the roaster as if this time she'd cooked it right. *More milk,* and she'd suddenly blush, forgetting, for a moment, the blonde and bowling and Wednesdays and legs. Congolese was what was really spoken, especially in the rain forests near the falls, but no one understood because they were too concerned with contemplating the merits of Flemish and French. *Belgisch Congo, Congo Belge,* I'd hear myself say softly over stamps, turning my head gently to the left three times like an exotic striped fish foraging silt. *Belgisch Congo, Congo Belge.* And the tribal crown of ostrich feathers. And zebras in foal. And full-bodied bosoms in carmine and slate. And blossoms dimmed by the night light in the hall coming velvet through cracked doors. And the touching beneath sheets for bamboo leaves or a spark. And spear splinters in the wet. And the unceasing equatorial heat.

CAVAFY'S CRAVING

Cavafy claimed he had become quite deaf. Something like a spur beneath the tongue when he read the indentations of snow in a cypress. Wind-blur in his belly, in leaves spoiling from the corpse's mouth, inside each cave-drawn burr in the cursive of the *History of Nikephoros Gregoras*.

And as for the oil lamp he carried from room to room those nights he searched for doves. And as for the tongue of a boy he longed to lull toward both of their dissolve. And for Constantinople constantly conspiring against his memory of Athens, even against the horror of his Aunt Martha's left breast accidentally exposed an evening moment, as she bent to scrub the stone floor in mashing light.

Trust. Not virtue. Lust. In the lack and length of his speculum of sperm, and all the ecstatic eel cravings like hot wax engraving the sheets. In his ears. Saddle soap of swaying stirrups. Inside his tormented fasts. And what a moth he held so thrumming shut against the closed fist of the world.

Deaf. Velvet. Sting beat of opium green with one dark eye widening in each wing. A burr beneath the tongue. His tongue, dead tongue. Alive with the ancestry of a cypress root in Athens. Constantine Cavafy's. Sung backward as a smalling toward song. Quite deaf. Quite breath. Quite ear hair curving his advancing age far back from the stirrup.

For love of stinging the world, Constantine Cavafy craved and wept and—he claimed—went deaf. And splayed his most private. Tongue split with spit, slung with dove-blood. Constant as Constantinople. Censer sway of smoiling leaves. Nile cloud in the smoke-taste trace. An unrequited tongue, or coming untucked as Aunt *this* or Uncle *that*. As the endless debate over the sensual merits of Athens or Alexandria. And the chance by lamplight at his writing table each night to chart a past. The chance to camphor from room to room an oil in the cave of his left ear, an accident of moths momentarily exposed far from the opium green of Athens. To stay alive. Another night. Constantly. To lie.

BRAHMS AND THE TAXIDERMIES OF SLEEP

She dreamed I had died, head-wound fate of a flight of stairs. When I woke, my leg was cramped, my breath uneasy and short. She had dreamed me into a cafe, sipping tea with Brahms, interrogating him about the violin that became a blind owlet in the third movement of the third symphony. He had suggested Russian tea with rose hips and cloves. I had argued the merits of curing a cello with salt.

I was scared enough to light a candle upon waking, she confided. I felt it singe some dark smear into my cheek when she bent her loose nightclothes over me, inspecting my skull, quietly fingering it so as not to wake me. *What really disturbed me,* she later admitted, *wasn't the snail curve of owl blood on the pillow, but the gills you had grown, how the candle made them fade. That, and Brahms, of course,* she continued. *At least until both he and that baton dissolved when I tilted hot wax into your left ear, saying, Shoo! Go home! Leave us both alone!*

CHRISTINE BOYKA KLUGE

Christine Boyka Kluge received the 1999 Frances Locke
Poetry Award from *The Bitter Oleander*, which featured her
work with an interview in the fall 2001 issue. She was
co-winner of The MacGuffin's "Short Short" competition in
1998. Her writing has appeared in *Arts & letters, Fine
Madness, Kestrel, LUNA, Quarterly West*, and other journals.
She is also a visual artist and children's writer. She lives
with her husband and two daughters in Westchester County,
New York. Her first book of poetry is forthcoming from The
Bitter Oleander Press in 2003.

ANGEL EATING SNOW

Out on the deck, an angel is eating snow. Again and again, she places fistfuls on her long, white tongue, and the glittering mounds disappear. He is irritated by the continual sound of her lips smacking; the noise interferes with his image of an afterworld purged of human frailties and desires. He notices that her pale eyebrows grow together above her sapphire eyes, like a pair of seagull wings soaring above two distant, watery planets. Her eyes are remote and cold, twin Earths entirely covered by oceans. Anything alive in them has surely drowned by now. She stares in at him through the glass doors, patient or bored, he can't tell. He never imagined an ending like this.

He wonders if January's accumulation has any flavor, if she enjoys the taste of snow or is merely thirsty. For her sake, he hopes for at least a hint of thawing maple buds or a mossy aftertaste. Although he is more tired than ever, although his body feels like a patchwork of cornhusks, he thinks he might like to try some snow, just to see for himself. He pushes up from the sagging green couch with his knobby arms and teeters toward the sliders. Three white carnations droop in a vase by the doors, wafting a cloud of sickly sweet perfume. Using both hands, he pulls the stubborn door along its track, and January wind blows away their stale scent of illness.

Outside, the annoying noise is even louder. He hears ice crystals crunching between her teeth and winces. When he scoops a handful of snow off the railing and puts it in his own mouth, she makes no comment. Without emotion, the angel watches him chew. Stubbornly, he watches her back. Up close, her flat face looks translucent and sleepy, blue crescents traced beneath her eyes. Although she seems old, there is not a single crease or wrinkle in her skin. She wears a long ivory nightgown that pulls at the seams. How had she grown so plump eating only snow? Something about her reminds him of his late wife. He'd like to rub his grizzled chin against her flannel nightie, rest his head on that familiar pillow of tummy. As he swallows, the snow melts and trickles in freezing runnels down his throat. It tastes like nothing, really, nothing at all.

A sudden, bitter gust of wind snaps the belt of his terrycloth robe against his chest. He looks down at the ends whipping back and forth like charmed snakes. Hypnotized for a moment, he fails to notice the angel tossing something over the picnic table. Like a meteor, it lands between his bare feet and sizzles. When the medallion bursts into flame, he bends down to examine it. The letters of his name coil in molten cursive letters across its surface, but he has forgotten how to read, doesn't recognize the token that will pay for a long journey in the company of this creature. Bewildered, he gingerly pinches the hot gold between his thumb and forefinger, already calculating how many chocolate kisses he can buy for his wife with this lucky coin.

WATCHING HER SOUL FROM BELOW

I can never tell if her soul is on backward or if it's just turned inside-out. I only see her at dusk, from a great distance, so I can't look for telltale silver snaps or pearly buttons. She was always ivory-skinned and faded-eyed, so she and her soul are all of a color anyway. I do see something that sparkles at her neck, like a locket winking gold in the last light, catching my eye over there on the ledge. She perches, swaying, flapping her white arms, and I can only watch, afraid to move. Because she doesn't want to leave yet, I hold her steady with my eyes. As the light dies, her cries are high and hollow, secret as a dog whistle, just for me. My ears prick to listen for words, but this language has none. With darkness, it disappears, like a voice pulled down a drain.

From below, her soul looks like a hospital gown, but iridescent. Maybe it's sewn from feathers, white ones with eyes, like albino peacock feathers. On windy evenings it whips around her like a blank silk flag, ready to take the name of any country, all colors of allegiance bleached or blown off over the escarpment. Her soul looks so loose, so slippery, that one night I am sure that a gust will twist and knot it into a pair of wings. They will snap free and soar over her head, leaving her with only her human body, clinging to the cliff edge with its brittle white claws.

NARCISSUS'S SUITCASE

Narcissus keeps his heart in a mirrored suitcase. He keeps the suitcase zipped and locked and chained to his bony wrist. The suitcase has little wheels; he brings it with him everywhere. Illuminated by a battery-powered night-light, the six inside mirrors reflect the heart seductively twittering on its glass pedestal. Through tiny peepholes, he monitors the speed of his heart's hypnotic pumping and the intensity of its blush. He sniffs at the glowing vent to gauge the proper iron level (the scent of rusted nails), and constantly touches the leather to check its temperature.

Shielding the box from bumps. Narcissus wanders the sidewalks, holding his heart hostage in its polished black mobile home. He makes his way in squiggly circles, always looking down, crossing the highway and bus routes and train tracks, again and again, until with a shiver, a leaf unfurls from his forehead. Until his callused feet take root in a crack in the cement, and his weakening arms bloom in delicate white petals.

The suitcase leaps the tracks and keeps on rolling, dragging its jangling leash.

BLACK PEARL

I'm sure she stumbled for miles in high school, that loss cutting into her sole like crushed glass in her shoe, until the drowning dulled and death glowed like a black pearl, pain's accretion of dark luster. She held out the pearl of her father's death like a prize, something we might be tempted to snatch, that kept us in a fascinated circle around her tear-stained face. Teenagers, we were hooked by this mystery and sadness, lured by the story of the tipped boat, the hole in the water he had vanished through.

We all leaned forward when she cried, alarmed by her face, puckered red and ugly as a neglected baby's. But we were drawn to that smoky pearl, grief's sharp-edged grit transformed to strange beauty. We all longed to touch its satin and shiver, but none of us wanted to hold the cold sphere within her own fist.

She looked up at us from our cafeteria table, as if she had dived to the dark bottom of the sea with her father, then alone dared to rise. The pearl of his last breath was cupped in her hands like an iridescent bubble of air, lifting her back to the surface, where light was captured in the water's crazed glass. Beyond that shattered pane, she searched for our soft, blurred faces looking down from their great height, from the safe, sunlit ledge she might never climb back to again.

JAR OF BEES

He stored his anger like a swarm of killer bees in a baby food jar, then hid the jar in the musty dumbwaiter at his core. The passageway under his ribs was dark and drafty, echoing with a warning buzz. Black static surrounded the space once occupied by an incandescent heart. Keeping his secret forced him to press his lips together in a chapped white line. Hives spread over his narrow chest in crimson Braille. Although his fingertips constantly traced the raised words beneath his shirt, he was afraid to decipher their furious message.

When his sister cried, he heard a pulley creak in his brain. He imagined frayed rope hoisting his jar up from a cellar kitchen, to be offered above like an exotic hors d'oeuvre, a quivering jar of gold caviar, both irresistible and fatal. They would unscrew the little blue dented lid, and…

He jumped up and down in front of the bathroom mirror, convinced he could shatter the jar. Squinting into fluorescent light, he searched his throat's rosy tunnel for bees, expecting them to explode from his innards like topaz shrapnel. None ever appeared; not one bee escaped. He wondered if a boy could be stung to death from the inside.

GIVING AWAY BONES

I stood at the corner giving away my bones. My ribs went to the little girl who needed a cage for her ferret. My toe bones went to a gambler to replace his unlucky dice. My spine went home coiled around the neck of a snake charmer. As I plucked out each one, I felt delightfully emptier, translucent as breath. I simply stepped out of my ivory corset.

The only piece I had trouble leaving was my skull. It stared at me with cavernous sockets like twin black wells. I appreciated the way it had cradled my brain, holding my thoughts in its bowl. But at last I kissed its brow, placing it on the desk of an artist, something to hold her bouquet of paintbrushes.

You might think my organs were left lonely and cold, but they were already gone by then—untangled, shriveled by sun, then pinkish-gray dust blown away on the wind. Inhaled by passing clouds. All that remained of me was something like a peeled mirror, a human image without dimension, distilled to particles of light. Like a paper doll, I turned sideways and disappeared.

I cherished my formless freedom. It was a game to avoid a new body. I loved the risk of riding in the space between the molecules of others' flesh, evading their grip. Except for a strange tickle along that narrow route, they hardly knew I was inside. I was as soft and slender as a laser beam, traveling at the speed of light.

Here I am, shimmering in the morning, air, hidden inside a scrap of fog. I could enter your fingertips, surprise you with new words, leave a drawing inside of your eyes. I'll knot a strand of myself like a ribbon around your soul, purr in electric circles around your quivering heart, switch your rhythm for my own.

My spirit will stretch to inhabit millions of bodies, not just one at a time, tie us all together with haloes of light—change the earth into my ball of silver thread.

HUMAN WITH LITTLE SUN IN HER HANDS

March morning, silent. Unexpected snow keeps coming, white clumps falling from trees like frozen apple blossoms. Seasonal confusion. Spring is out there, somewhere, approaching. Today there are four crows again, wary, even after all of these offerings. We keep a respectful distance. They wait, two each on two branches, then land on the railing. Go back to the tree. Return to the railing. Each time they move, more white flowers drift down. Eyes and beaks glitter. In these moments, the snow's music changes from empty hiss to the wet sounds of the roof dripping, of invisible runnels coursing under snow. The porous membrane between seasons is leaking. I want to capture this with my camera. One picture left. Last time, last storm, the snow falling at night made exploding stars in the camera's flash. I want to see what happens when the flash catches flakes and black feathers in daylight. Crusts wait, scattered on a bench, like meteorites deep in craters of snow. Louder dripping. Still snowing, just sparse. Large feather-flakes twirl past. Crows call. Not moving, they stare at me, the human with a little sun in my hands. I'm sure the picture won't come out. The crows won't come close enough, not while the camera covers my face like a black mask.

ANATOMY WOMAN ESCAPES

Anatomy Woman escapes from her metal shelf, leaping three floors from the open lab window. As she falls, she looks out from her transparent head with two blue marbles, greedily observing the autumn garden. Chrysanthemums ripple yellow to rust, and the sky is the color of chicory. In the oak, a blue jay flashes sparks from branch to branch.

She lands planted up to her ankles in emerald moss. Inside a torso of crazed glass, her heart becomes a greenhouse rose, tangled in brambles of blue and red vessels. But no fragrance can emanate from its quivering petals, trapped in her body's glass house. Perplexed yellow jackets wander the cracks above her ribs like spilled bronze beads. She can't feel them, only the fire of October sun, withering velvet bloom to parchment. This freedom is a terrible beauty. Through the crackling skin other raised fist, she sees with brittle clarity the jagged edge of the clutched stone.

A crimson leaf adheres to her chest like a hand on a broken window.

THE CHALK BRIDE

The chalk bride climbs the last thousand steps of the spiral staircase to the glowing ballroom. She is snowing; the surface of her fragile body twists and drifts in crystal flakes. When she finally places her wasted feet on the marble floor, the luminous groom drops from a cloud on the ceiling, startling her by pressing his ivory lips to her lacy neck. This snowman kiss draws him into her personal blizzard, and they spin like a chandelier in a gust, a double-helix of confetti-light.

While the caged wind whistles through its teeth, wallflower angels hum along. Shed flakes form sugar-coating on their iridescent shoulders. They sound like bees, sluggish from cold. On the crumbling edges of the dance floor, icicle ghosts sway and drip to the faint music. Frozen breaths fill the room with white balloons that shimmer and rise, then shrink into blurred constellations.

Now roofless, the expanding room becomes a floating veil of snow, numb white-on-white. This pale waltz must be *HEAVEN,* where the borders of bodies are stirred and erased. When the particles of their minds collide, the swirling couple forgets if this is the first dance or the last. Together, they have faith that once the storm clears, the view from this height will stretch forever.

ALL OF ITS WORDS, BOTH WINGED AND QUILLED

The best poems have a steady wind blowing through them, a low, haunting howl you can almost hear. The wind threatens to lift the surface world like a rock, releasing the scent of damp soil, exposing the scurrying, chewing things beneath. When I start to read a great poem, I'm at the edge of a dark opening, letting my eyes adjust, curious. Cold air rushes up through my hair. Water from stalactites plinks into a distant underground stream. I'm suddenly alert, skin prickled and shivery.

Entering its cave, I expect to find a pile of gnawed bones, or feel a moist palm on the back of my neck. Musk announces the presence of something alive inside its passages, something stronger and wilder than narrow words can restrain—a leathery, immortal creature, a giant draped in the humid rags of a subterranean realm. What lurks inside the poem, singing to me, is so rare, that, at first, my face lifts with wonderment. I recognize the voice of the beast that dwells there, precious last of its kind.

But on the cusp of delighted laughter, my features twist, puzzled. I sense something clinging to my arm in the dark—affectionate, intimate—but with glistening teeth. I'm poised to bolt, but the spell of its throaty new language is on my own tongue like an elixir. Enchanted, I want it to whisper its life's story in my ear. I long to savor all of its words, both winged and quilled. Trustingly, gently, I run my fingers up and down the black pearls of its spine. Its amber eyes are the only dim lights. I stare into the dilated pupils, unafraid, willing to place my head in its jaws.

MARY KONCEL

Mary Koncel is the author of two books of prose poems—
Closer to Day (Quale Press, 1999), a chapbook; and a full
collection, *You Can Tell The Horse Anything* (Tupelo Press,
2003). Her prose poems have appeared in many journals,
including *The Massachusetts Review, The Prose Poem: An
International Journal, key satch(el)* and *Denver Quarterly*, and in
the anthology *The Party Train: A Collection of North American
Prose Poetry.* (New Rivers Press, 1995). In 1996, she received
a poetry grant from the Massachusetts Cultural Council. In
addition to being a freelance writer, she teaches writing at
Smith College and lives in Worthington, Massachusetts.

THE LAKE SHORE LIMITED

The conductor crawls into my lap. Resting his head against my shoulder, he sucks his thumb, rolls back his eyes, and calls me "mother."

It is times like this that I regret. I am not his mother. He is a short, bald man from Akron, Ohio. I could never sing him midnight lullabies or offer him a breast full of pure mother's milk. "Go away," I whisper in the soft, fleshy folds of his ears.

My husband returns from the bathroom, proud hips swaying with the train's steady rhythm. Unwrapping a package of cigars, he lights the thickest one and places it between the conductor's lips. "My son," he says before taking his seat next to me and the mounds of corn stalks that push and groan outside the window.

Across the aisle, a woman points a donut at us, smiles, then begins a telegram. "How perfect," she writes, "a man, a woman, and their son—the bald conductor from Akron, Ohio."

I shake my head, but my husband and the conductor agree. They stare, as if expecting me to throw open my arms and take each passenger. It's all so strange. The rumble of the train, the quiet blur of towns, this pale black halo of motherhood that looms above my head.

COME BACK, ELVIS, COME BACK TO HOLYOKE

They still love you, Elvis. They want your hair, stories about your Harley ripping up pavement between Nashville and Memphis, your sequined gaze, your big-breasted women in too-tight bikinis. "Teacher," they say to me, "Make us walk and talk like Elvis."

I tell them you're dead, fat, bloated, overweight and dead. But Juan Carlos insists that you live below him, that you stir steaming pots of black beans while singing "Maria Encantadora" on the radio every Tuesday. And Clarence calls you Father.

These boys need you, Elvis. Every day they sit, shaping their lips and grinding their hips beneath the desks. Across the room, I watch them, see little birds, baby roosters, dull voiced peacocks with bare chests and tender white throats.

Elvis, I'm only a woman. I can't do it all. I'm only a woman, and they're asking more questions. When I stand up, they point at me, stare at the split of my skirt, the breasts beneath the sheen of my blouse.

Next time, forget the supermarkets in Denver, the trailer park in Lafayette. Come back to Holyoke. Teach these boys to be men, great manly men, men that love women, red meat, and '56 Fords. Elvis, like the streets of Holyoke, my arms open to you, wait for you, your low lean rumble.

THE NEIGHBORHOOD MAN

A dog is rolling in the grass. A man walks by and thinks the dog is drowning. But the man's not sure because he's just a neighbor. The dog is very convincing, turning over and over, its long legs kicking up clumps of grass. The man strips off his suit, drops to his knees, and rolls in after the dog. He hopes the dog can hold on just a while longer.

The man is having problems. He's getting very tired, barely able to keep his head above the grass. It's very late. He hopes this will be over soon. But the dog is getting smaller, the grass much deeper.

mundane
moments
turned
absurd!

BUMP

When I hit a bump in the road, I never think bump. I think poor, big man lying in the middle of the road. And once again I've hit him, flattened him good, all four wheels, dead center. I'm headed home. It's always dark. Sometimes rainy. I say, "Oh dear, not again." This poor man should be asleep in his red chaise lounge. His fried chicken dinner half eaten, and he settled in for the evening, his mother knitting beside him, a cat or two licking their tails.

I think if only it was a bump, a huge unrepentant swelling of pavement. If only, minutes before, the man told his mother, "I think I'll read a book tonight. Sit here in my red chaise lounge." A bump would be so much simpler. No pity. No remorse. And his mother so much like mine.

Now she's alone. She's wishing her son through the front door, past the telephone table, across the blue flecked linoleum. How much he loves her chicken. Who wouldn't? Especially the wings and thighs.

Then there's the road. It's no help. "Screw the man," it tells me in the wet, raspy voice of a road. Still I bite my lip as I try to remember back, sort the bumps from the men, the men from the bumps.

ON WEEPING ICONS

Across Sheffield Avenue, another bus pulls up. My mother greets the hordes of faithful, ushers them up the stairs, presses them into deep wooden pews. Today the lampata is especially bright, and Mary is weeping inside a dingy red church on the near north side of Chicago.

I ponder this. As I walk across my pasture, between another spring and fat ponies kicking through the last morning hour, I think about fence posts and weeping icons. "They're hungry for tears," my mother writes. "They want their miracles—hair, plump babies, a tide of untouched sleep."

Her job is simple. Taking the old babas first, she folds them into the small nest of her arms, carries their fleshy souls to Mary. Together, they are grateful. Now there are lips softened by sturdy prayer, incense warming the vestibule.

The children must be taught. Their knees are pink and restless. They forget how to cross themselves. Like the stern, but loving fists of God, my mother is always patient. She explains again why Mary, Theotokas, Virgin Mother of this Befuddled Earth, has given herself in streams of tears.

Sometimes I too am hungry. And I still remember how to kneel, fold my fingers and cross myself, right to left. But this morning. Mother, you should know that tall trees flicker, taut and certain, that bare, wild hooves can rise up as if in blesséd flight.

LOVE POEM

Nearly midnight, a man and a woman lie in bed—the man thinking of dented hubcaps, a hand spinning out of control, breath clear as gasoline and the woman thinking of her cat.

It's nothing kinky. It's just that the cat knows how to have a good time. A fat orange tabby prowling down alleys, trash cans and doorways standing at bay as he hunts for his kind of love, a loud vernacular love. And everywhere the slight blue hum of moonlight.

The woman could easily follow, get down on all fours and leap off the windowsill, learn to arch her back like a bitch in heat. She could get used to that.

Of course, the cat is oblivious. He stops, rubs against his shadow, stretches one thick leg then another before deciding north or south. Tonight, he's looking good. After all it's summer—flagrant stars, a toiling sky and the smell of life moving on.

If only the man would turn. If only he would reach beneath the sheets and find the warmth of thigh. If only the man would be a man. Tired, the woman slowly drifts off to sleep. Another stupid sleep, she tells herself, the room and its darkness aching around her.

THE YEAR OF THE MAN

My friends aren't hungry anymore. When they walk down streets, they belch and rub their fat, slick bellies. "You, you, and you," they say, pointing their fingers as if sorting Buicks from Fords, left feet from right ones.

These men are looking pretty good. And it's not even spring. It's the year of the man. Before it was a drought, a drought on top of a drought. Now they're dropping from trees, sprouting through cracks, littering parks and alleys like empty bottles or dented cans.

And my poor, poor husband! Every night he dreams he's a windswept virgin stranded on a ragged cliff in some dark, undeclared country. "What does it mean?" he asks me. "What does it mean?' I tell him about the sad old days, about big vacant beds and the song of the drought, that long, long drought. And always, of course, I tell him, "Sure, I want you, I need you," over and over.

Last week even Peggy called me. Whispering, "It smells a little fleshy today," she abruptly hung up. I stepped out on my porch and breathed, letting beads of sweat and full ripe muscles fill my lungs. "Yes," I wrote back three days later, "the sweet still scent of thigh."

MEDITATION ON A BIRD SITTING ON A MAN'S HEAD

Not really. It's about the man. He's sleeping on a bench, beneath some leaves and a scorched morning sky. The bird is big, a pigeon perhaps. As the man lifts a hand across his cheek like a wing, children squat in a water fountain, and a red sun beats above him. No wonder he's dreaming of birds.

In some countries, a sleeping man and his bird are considered good luck. The man woken up, given a robe, a stick, and three barrels of corn. After the bird is captured and dressed like a boy child, the man is asked to repeat the Dream of the Bird in foreign tongues.

This man's dream begins with damp feathers. His friends call him Omar, Om for short. After circling mounds of shifting sand, he swoops down and grabs a fish from the shoulder of a well-wrapped peasant. He eats, hungry for bone but not remembering pebbles or their dabbling streams.

And later? Who knows. Wind and a coarsely uttered song?

The man rolls over, mumbles into his sleeve. This summer has been long, and the bird is peeking through his hair. Poor man. Poor, tired sleeping man, lips drawn, eyes fluttering behind crusted lids as if measuring distance, discovering nest.

WHEN THE BABIES ARE MISSING AGAIN

We don't even look for them. We're tired. It's Friday night, and across the living room, the man on the TV stares at us, past everyone, at us. "It's 11 o'clock. Do you know where your babies are?" We shake our heads, shrug. No. When the babies are missing, they won't be found. They wear leather jackets, sometimes wool caps. They drink, smoke, hunker behind telephone booths or trees, kiss with open lips and fat baby tongue. (They've whispered this to us. When they're home. When they've tucked themselves in blankets, sucking their thumbs, eyes rolling back with incoming sleep.) "Damn those babies," we want to say, but we don't dare. The man on the TV waits, his mouth a pink shade of expectation, a puff of disbelief. What can we tell him? That the babies hardly ever swear. That they eat their bowls of green beans and squash. We think, *How to begin.*

THE SECOND SONG OF INSOMNIA

A stranger is humming outside my window. He looks like my dead uncle or a drunk angel in rubber boots and a baggy wool overcoat. I'm just not sure. I'm easily confused by that black spot of moustache that shimmers in the half moon air.

But every night this stranger follows me home. He leans against the tree, taking for granted my grass, the staggered line of streetlights, this curtain that separates me from a deep husky sleep. Now he's rolled up his sleeves. I watch his lips, but he's too clever, his mute breath lingering inside my head like a dream, like a bad dream running over and over.

It's not right for a stranger to be humming outside my window. He should go home. He should read books, big red books, and let me close my eyes. Listen. I need words, even simple words. I won't apologize. I want a song, a really nice song, with words that grab my heart and swing it dizzily around this room, then drop me into some midnight abyss. Instead I find myself pressed between these sheets, throat aching in my hands, waiting for the first howl of a hungry dog, the rise of footsteps, something that brings night closer to day.

MORTON MARCUS

Morton Marcus is the author of numerous books of poetry,
including *Pages From a Scrapbook of Immigrants* (Coffee House
Press, 1988), *When People Could Fly* (Hanging Loose Press,
1997), *Moments Without Names: New and Selected Prose Poems*
(White Pine Press, 2002) *Shouting Down the Silence* (Creative
Arts Books, 2002), and *Bear Prints: Collected Verse Poems*
(Creative Arts, 2003). He taught Film and Literature at
Cabrillo College in Aptos, California, until his retirement in
1998. He lives in Santa Cruz, California.

THE WORDS

When we sleep, the words inside us slide from their hiding places like thieves and assassins in a Renaissance city.

It is after midnight, but there are all these figures, muffled in cloaks or slipping from one pillar to another in black capes, who whisper and bicker, or come upon one another unexpectedly in the dark.

One stabs another in a shadowy arcade, and leaves the body where it falls. At the edge of a piazza, four ruffians, growling and cursing, carry off a drunken student in a burlap sack.

The facades of townhouses are still and dark, although whimpers and sighs and raspy snores flutter from the partially open windows, their meanings blurred by the fountains burbling in the squares.

The quiet everywhere is stippled by these sounds, as if the buildings were restless and muttering.

A shout. Lights flare at windows. Torches dot a piazza. It seems the body has been discovered.

But the sounds are confused, the reports garbled. Is it war, disease, the birth of an heir in the prince's palace?

A bell booms in a cathedral tower. The sound rushes in all directions over the tile rooftops.

A mile or two down the road leading to the city's west gate, a peasant in a cart lets his donkey guide him home as he sings of love, death and the joys of a simple life.

THE 8TH, 9TH, AND 10TH WONDERS OF THE WORLD

In the midst of a civil war, two men were arrested in different sections of the same city and summarily sentenced to be executed the next morning.

One of the men had been a spy and blown up a barracks, killing twenty soldiers. The other had done nothing, but his protestations of innocence had gone unheeded by his captors.

Both men spent their last night in the same cell. The cell, which had been the basement of a family home before the war, smelled of urine and goats. It contained no lights and no furniture, and the two men sat in the dark on the straw-strewn stone floor, exchanging small talk about their lives and listening to the howitzers thumping on the hills above the city and the small arms fire occasionally stuttering through the streets.

Suddenly the spy blurted out with a bitter laugh, "They say there are seven wonders of the world—the Hanging Gardens at Babylon, the Lighthouse at Pharos, the Great Wall of China. But these are all things men have built, physical things, and almost every one of them has disappeared like dust in the wind, as we will tomorrow. "I tell you this: there is an eighth wonder, my friend, and it is the human imagination. We can conceive of anything—not just those seven constructions, but a warm willing woman who will love us when we are lonely, a good meal when we are hungry, and a successful end to this war, when we will finally be at peace and our people in power.

"That is what keeps me going and that is why I blew up the barracks—and that is why I am not afraid to die."

His voice shivered away in the darkness.

The innocent man shifted on the straw but didn't reply. His face was covered with shadows and the spy couldn't see his expression.

They sat in silence for several minutes. Then the innocent man began to speak with great difficulty in a small voice, as if struggling to find the words for his thoughts. "I don't know. I was thinking as you spoke that there had to be something beyond the imagination. I'm not sure, but maybe it is the fact that somewhere along the line those who have taken me from my wife and children and condemned me to die will be forgiven.

"If I cannot forgive them, maybe my wife will, or my children, or my children's children. I mean, hatred cannot go on forever.

"And when it occurred to me just now that all of us contain this capacity to forgive, I said to myself, 'If the imagination is the eighth wonder of the world, surely forgiveness is the ninth.'"

"I'll agree to that," exclaimed the spy with a snicker, "if you agree that the tenth wonder is our capacity to forget."

MY FATHER'S HOBBY

My father's hobby—don't laugh—was collecting sneezes. No stamps or coins for him. "The stuff of life," he said, "of life."

My mother and brothers shook their heads, his friends smirked, but he hurt no one, was an honest electrician, and everyone eventually shrugged it off as a harmless quirk. As his closest friend, Manny Borack, told my mom, "It could be worse."

Dad would mount the sneezes on glass slides he carried in his pockets everywhere he went. Some sneezes resembled flower petals, others seafoam, amoebas, insect wings, still others fan-shaped fingerless foetal hands, splatters of raindrops, or empty cocoons.

Next he stained the specimens magenta, turquoise, egg-yolk yellow, and placed them in the glass cases that stood in all the rooms.

Late at night when the family slept, he'd arrange handfuls of the slides on the light table in his study, and, switching off the lamp, he would peer down at them and smile.

One night, a small boy with bad dreams, I crept terrified through the darkened house to the study. He was bent over his collection, his face, surrounded by darkness, glowing in the table's light, as his lips murmured something again and again.

I slid my small hand into his and listened. He was rocking back and forth, bowing to the slides. "God bless you," he was saying, "God bless."

THE GIRL WHO BECAME MY GRANDMOTHER

Every night after the household was asleep, the girl who became my grandmother rode her stove through the forests of Lithuania.

She would return by dawn, her black hair gleaming with droplets of dew and her burlap sack filled with fog-webbed mushrooms and roots.

"It's true," my grandfather said. "At first I followed, but I could never keep up." He would hear the clanging and rusty squeakings fade into the trees and, with a sigh, he would go home.

He accepted the situation until the night she left in the kitchen, as if she were riding in a coach pulled by black horses of wind.

Grandfather followed in the rest of the house, standing in the doorway to the now-departed room, bellowing threats as if urging the house forward at greater speed.

He caught her outside Vilna, when she stopped to get her bearings, and the house slammed into the stalled kitchen, grandfather tumbling through the doorway and hitting his head on the leg of a table.

"And where do you think you're going this time, Lady?" he groaned from the floor, rubbing his right ear.

The girl smiled down at him and, kneeling by his side, stroked his hair, but didn't say anything.

That was the last time the girl who became my grandmother went on a nocturnal outing. Soon after, they left for America.

In Brooklyn, she rode from one day to the next in the house he had built around her, watching the changing scene beyond the kitchen window.

It was then she became my grandmother, white-haired and smiling, never saying much of anything, even when the old man shouted from the other rooms. Not that he ever needed anything. He just wanted to be sure she was still there.

SMOKING CIGARS

When I smoke a cigar, I'm part of the earth again, but a wilder earth than municipal parks and public gardens. The wrapped brown leaves, brittle as autumn, smell like rotting fish and crumbling stone.

Even in an apartment high above the city, I become an element of the earth once more, when the cigar smoke enfolds me like the air inside a tomb.

I sit at a table opposite an empty chair when I smoke, and imagine the cigar is an earthen whistle through which I summon whatever ghost will come. Most of the time it's a leathery man, his skin as brown and thin as tobacco leaves.

We sit face to face across the table, not speaking, smoking the same cigar from opposite directions, my mouth clasping the unlit end, and his the fiery cinder whose glow must resemble the burning coal that sprang from the darkness to start the world.

He blows into the cigar as if blowing on the coal, and I suck until I am filled with the life beyond this one. When I exhale, he sips my living air through the pink nipple that scorches his tongue.

In church on Sundays, some people eat and drink the body and blood of their god. I consort with those who are less sublime, the ones who built the pyramids and tombs with their hands, and who vanished without hope of being revered or even remembered.

MOON & FLOWER

for Djuro Radovic

Moon and flower: a lilting breeze, the pale, reflected moonlight washing over the stone flower.

My wife and I went there, high up, thousands of feet over the bare mountains into sun-parched uplands all limestone and under-brush: white, gray, sand-colored rocks, and the tough shrubs gripping down, the dusty bushes, the dry creepers and spiraling cypress trees—stunted, crippled shapes holding fast year after year against sun and wind: so high and otherworldly, my mind swam beyond the precipices of time and space.

And finally—over stone roads, lanes really, immemorial tracks winding past forgotten walls of piled rock and occasional farms holding on as stubbornly as the vegetation around them—we arrived at this wind-lashed cemetery where stone grave-lids, ten-foot long rectangular slabs, were scattered about like lichen-spotted dominoes the gods had played with and abandoned eons before.

In one corner, past brambles and briars, stood a gray stone five feet across and six feet high, its front and back surfaces carved with lines of skirted figures dancing arm in arm among birds and horses and other half-formed animals, its narrow sides incised with strange hieroglyphs on one end, and on the other a crescent moon rising over a stone flower.

No one is sure who placed the stone there a thousand years ago or more, carved the indecipherable words, and chiseled the childlike figures who century after century have continued to perform their jubilant dance.

"Moon and flower," said Djuro, the friend who drove us there, pointing to the stone and then to the scattered grave-lids. "Look on new grave here: one grave, two grave, all—you see? Is symbol now—moon and flower—everywhere in valley."

"Moon and flower," my wife murmured, the people long settled in this place—family we'd come to visit—as much her people as Djuro's. "Moon and flower," she repeated. "What does it mean?"

"No one know. People come—my peoples, yours—and see and make it symbol. A mystery. These peoples long gone, finished," and he brushed his palms together as if ridding them of dust.

My peoples. The way he said it—the set of his jaw, the pride in his voice—the three of us understood he was not only referring to the inhabitants of those mountains and the valley we'd driven from, but also to their doggedly rebuilding this land after the third foreign invasion in less than a hundred years.

But why the moon and flower? Did these people recognize in it a forgotten ancestral memory that triggered an urge in them to resurrect it as a symbol, or was it merely the suggested softness of the flower that attracted them, the gentle illumination of the moon, the evocation I had just heard in my wife's voice of peaceful evenings that all of us in one way or another hope to secure?

Tonight, quiet, having contemplated all evening the ends of empire—palaces and skyscrapers toppling over the precipice of time—and having been moved to melancholy by the moonlight beyond the window, I thought of the standing stone high in the moonlight of that other place thousands of miles away, and imagined a breeze slipping over the crescent moon and the stone flower and then passing over the skirted figures, who in their place on top of the world, night after night, year after year, their movements open only to the gaze of the blind universe, continue to dance.

ANGEL INCIDENT

An angel appeared in my study not too long ago: bedraggled, mussed hair, muttering to himself. Both wings lifted like ocean swells with every breath he drew or word he spoke. They seemed to have a life of their own; I couldn't take my eyes off them.

The angel kept muttering to himself. He was studying a crumpled, poorly folded map, the kind bought at gas stations: he opened panels and refolded them, peering repeatedly at the network of lines inside.

He knew I was there. Several times he looked up and smiled weakly—I nodded in reply—but he never asked me directions before he strolled through the wall near the window and was gone.

Of course, I never asked him if he needed help. It never occurred to me. At the time, I thought it was enough that we were in the same room together. I was wrong. We both were.

GOODBYE TO THE TWENTIETH CENTURY

Goodbye, Mother. Don't feel guilty. You didn't let us down; we let you down. You existed only for us, and we responded to your pampering and protectiveness by destroying almost everything that came within our grasp. And now with few regrets, most of us turn our backs on you and leave you behind.

You had such hopes, such ambitions for us, and we disappointed you. Now you sit, a palsied old woman hunched in the corner of the kitchen, hardly more than a large shadow hovering on the wall, watching us, it must seem, celebrating your death, behaving like children concerned only with the party ahead, as we continually glance at the door on the day we finally leave home.

Don't be despondent. At the stroke of midnight, the house won't become a pumpkin rotting in a field. The instant the tower clock tolls twelve, the house will transform into a museum, which will carry in its depths the mementos and bric-a-brac of the century, like those children's rooms that mothers keep exactly as they were before the children left home for good.

And what a museum it will be—large enough to house biplanes with canvas wings, zeppelins and B-17s, jet fighters and rockets, and a complete collection of antique cars. Entire wings of the museum will be devoted to fashions in clothes and hairdos, and others to all sorts of weaponry. Exhibition halls will be dedicated to toys and games, portrait galleries to photographs of prime ministers and athletes and movie stars, and room after room to instruments of torture and to dioramas of plaster animals posed among exotic trees, all now extinct. Many of the exhibits will be painful reminders, to be sure—but at least some of your children and grandchildren will come to visit on weekends and rainy days.

And of those visitors, some, perhaps, will be curious, and stroll thoughtfully from room to room, and maybe they will come upon the chamber that sits in the center of the museum, surrounded by all the other rooms and connecting halls, like a throne room in the middle or a maze. You know the room, the one that glows in the darkness and is filled with display cases stretching into the shadows on all sides. Each case contains not butterflies but dreams in many shapes and hues, iridescent pinks and golds and blues that retain their brilliance and seem to wait in breathless slumber, as if they would take wing at the slightest prodding, flying from those glass cases that every hundred years are transported from the depths of one museum to another.

THE FACE

I was slick with sweat and panting from hillsides, and had knelt to drink from the sun-wrinkled surface of the River Usk, when I saw my face staring back at me from the sliding water.

The face was transparent, lidded by tree-shade and clouds overhead, and the head behind it was hollow, filled with fish as fine as feathers and stones stuck in bottom mud.

Who was this, so clearly me surprised to come upon myself looking back into my face with a face that was as surprised as mine was?

It was me gone back to stones and mud, the self removed from the seeing eye, looking back at an observer who couldn't imagine what the other face beheld.

The river rolled and wrinkled by, but the face held fast, as if staring from behind a window. It was imprisoned by my watching it, as I was imprisoned by its watching me.

I stared, and it stared back. Then I bent to the water and kissed as much as drank the face, and the water channeled through me, a branching coldness like the fingers of a hand reaching out and holding on.

Even before I rose, I knew the water's surface would splinter and shake and reform into the sliding river, sun-wrinkled and expressionless once again.

I make no claim beyond the telling. I left that place no wiser than before, but carrying a second self who has swayed within me ever since—silent, self-contained, waiting beneath every breath I draw.

THE PEOPLE WE NEVER HEARD OF

Where did they go, the people we never heard of?

Did they build those sandstone monuments that slump in the desert or crumble in the tightening web of jungle vines?

Not the Egyptians or Mayans or the people who inhabited Angkor Wat, but the ones we never heard of, who came like a wind through the passes, fluttered into this valley or that, and were gone, leaving humps in the land, maybe a rock formation here and there, and utensils whose markings we cannot decipher.

If matter can neither be created nor destroyed, the people we never heard of are still here, just over that hill, where we can't see them, or behind our eyes, where their presence is a pressure we intuit more than understand.

I mean, do we lift a spoon, tie a knot, smile and weep as we do because those people did it first, showing us how?

A thousand years from now when this planet is a single city and the oceans are ponds in a system of municipal parks, will our descendants come across our markings for trees and whales, unable to decipher them, and sense a pressure building behind their eyes and a longing rolling through their chests for things they no longer have words for, things irrevocably gone?

CAMPBELL MCGRATH

Campbell McGrath is the author of five books of poetry,
including *Spring Comes to Chicago* (1996), *Road Atlas* (l999)
and *Florida Poems* (2002), all published by The Ecco Press.
His awards include The Kingsley Tufts Prize and fellowships
from The Guggenheim and MacArthur Foundations. He
teaches in the creative writing program at Florida
International University in Miami.

THE PROSE POEM

On the map it is precise and rectilinear as a chessboard, though driving past you would hardly notice it, this boundary line or ragged margin, a shallow swale that cups a simple trickle of water, less rill than rivulet, more gully than dell, a tangled ditch grown up throughout with a fearsome assortment of wild-flowers and bracken. There is no fence, though here and there a weathered post asserts a former claim, strands of fallen wire taken by the dust. To the left a cornfield carries into the distance, dips and rises to the blue sky, a rolling plain of green and healthy plants aligned in close order, row upon row upon row. To the right, a field of wheat, a field of hay, young grasses breaking the soil, filling their allotted land with the rich, slow-waving spectacle of their grain. As for the farmers, they are, for the most part, indistinguishable: here the tractor is red, there yellow; here a pair of dirty hands, there a pair of dirty hands. They are cultivators of the soil. They grow crops by pattern, by acre, by foresight, by habit. What corn is to one, wheat is to the other, and though to some eyes the similarities outweigh the differences it would be as unthinkable for the second to commence planting corn as for the first to switch over to wheat. What happens in the gully between them is no concern of theirs, they say, so long as the plough stays out, the weeds stay in the ditch where they belong, though anyone would notice the wind-sewn cornstalks poking up their shaggy ears like young lovers run off into the bushes, and the kinship of these wild grasses with those the farmer cultivates is too obvious to mention, sage and dun-colored stalks hanging their noble heads, hoarding exotic burrs and seeds, and yet it is neither corn nor wheat that truly flourishes there, nor some jackalopian hybrid of the two. What grows in that place is possessed of a beauty all its own, ramshackle and unexpected, even in winter, when the wind hangs icicles from the skeletons of briars and small tracks cross the snow in search of forgotten grain; in the spring the little trickle of water swells to welcome frogs and minnows, a muskrat, a family of turtles, nesting doves in the verdant grass; in summer it is a thoroughfare for raccoons and opossums, field mice, swallows and black birds, migrating egrets, a passing fox; in autumn the geese avoid its abundance, seeking out windrows of toppled stalks, fatter grain more quickly discerned, more easily digested. Of those that travel the local road, few pay that fertile hollow any mind, even those with an eye for what blossoms, vetch and timothy, early forsythia, the fatted calf in the fallow field, the rabbit running for cover, the hawk's descent from the lightning-struck tree. You've passed this way yourself many times, and can tell me, if you would, do the formal fields end where the valley begins, or does everything that surrounds us emerge from its embrace?

THE GULF

Floating in the gulf, on a hot June day, listening to the seashells sing.

Eyes open I watch their migrations, their seismic shifts and tidal seizures, as I am seized and lifted, lulled and hushed and serenaded. Eyes closed, I drift amid their resonant sibilance, soft hiss and crackle in the tide wash, ubiquitous underwater, a buzz like static, or static electricity—but not mechanical—organic and musical, metallic as casino muzak, piles of change raked together, a handful of pennies down a child's slide. Eyes open I see them rise as one with the water, climbing the ridge with the incoming surge and then, released, called back, slide slowly down the face of their calcified escarpment, the sandy berm the small rippling waves butt up against and topple over—flop, whoosh—a fine wash of shells and shell bits and shards, a slurry of coquinas and scallops and sunrays, coral chunks, tubes and frills, the volute whorls of eroded whelks, a mass of flinty chips and nacreous wafers, singing as it descends. Like mermaids, singing. But not a song. Stranger and more varied, more richly textured, many-timbred, Gregorian hymns or aboriginal chanting, the music of pygmies in a forest clearing, complex, symphonic, indecipherable. But not human. Elemental. Like rain. Bands of tropical rain approaching from the jungle, sweeping the tile verandah, the sheet metal roof, against the slats of the louvered window and across the floor of storm light and coffee-flavored dust—but not liquid—mineral—mountains of shattered porcelain, broken bottles en route to the furnace—but not glass and not rain and not even a rain of glass. Ice. The day after the ice storm, when the sun peeks out, and wind comes off the lake, and what has so beautifully jeweled the trees all morning breaks loose in a sequence of tumbling cascades, chiming like tumbrels and lost castanets, falling upon snow-covered cars and encrusted fences, discarded Christmas trees piled up in the alley, smelling of wet balsam, string and plastic in their hair, and forgotten tinsel, and every needle encased in a fine translucent sheath of ice, and as I reach to touch them my fingers brush the sand and my knees bump the bottom and I am called back with a start, alien, suspended, wholly conceived within that other music, body in the water like the water in the flesh and the liquid in the crystal and the crystal in the snowflake and the mind within the body like the branch within its skin of ice.

Eyes open. Eyes closed.

Floating in the gulf, listening to seashells, thinking of the Christmas trees in the back-alleys of Chicago.

MOUNTAINAIR, NEW MEXICO

Stopped for lunch after crossing the Malpais, that awful wasteland, desolate, sun-stricken, palpably grievous. Eyeless window sockets in the town of Claunch; the ruined pueblo at Gran Quivíra. At the next table folks were talking about the unusual cold of the previous winter, so much snow a bear had come down from the mountains and roamed around town for days seeking shelter. "You remember that bear?" *Oh yeah, yeah. It was living over by Dale's place.* Lunch arrived—egg salad, pickles, iced tea. The door of the diner swung open and a man in spurs and chaps and stetson hat strode in, knocked the dust from his britches, sidled up to the old wooden bar and ordered a glass of milk. It came, full and frothy. The cowboy drank it, wiped his lips on his sleeve, paid, and left. At the next table they were still going at it. "Whatever happened to that bear?" *Dale shot it.* "He shot it? Killed it?" *Yep.* "Is that legal—killing a bear?" *I don't know, but he sure did shoot it.*

FOUR CLOUDS LIKE THE IRISH IN MEMORY

First memory of school: sitting in the grass beneath a blossoming dogwood tree while the teacher explains how to write a poem.

Boisterous sun, orbital crab apples, isn't the springtime beautiful? What do the clouds look like? Butterfly, banana split, polar bear, clown. What does the dogwood look like, its bracts and tiers and white cascades of flowers? Snowflakes. A birthday cake. Good, good. Like going to New York for the holidays, like heaven or the George Washington Bridge at night, its titanium spans and whirligigs, garlands of popcorn, garlands of cranberries, baked ham and my grandfather's accordion, my mother and her sisters trying out their old Shirley Temple routines amidst an Irish stew of relatives and well-wishers immersed for the day in the nostalgic mist and manners of the old sod.

Shamrock, whiskey bottle, subway train, diaspora.

One year my grandfather drove with us back to Washington after Christmas. I remember him chiefly for that matchless accordion, the hats and boats he made from newspaper, the senility that claimed him like an early snowfall—

as I remember my father's father for the crafty wooden puzzles he assembled at the kitchen table with a box of Ritz crackers and a quart of Rheingold beer

but this was my mother's father, a countryman from Donegal, famous for long strolls in Riverside Park collecting weeds for home remedies, for walking the bridge to save a penny on a pack of cigarettes. He worked forty years as a ticket taker in the subway, pent too long 'mid cloisters dim, and somewhere in southern New Jersey, in the backseat of the station wagon looking out past the turnpike traffic, he said, in his thick brogue, to no one in particular, *goodness,*

I had no idea there were such great forests left.

A DOVE

If May is the month of the mockingbird, September is the season of the dove. On the roof they have gathered to drink from warm puddles of yesterday's rainwater, preening and cooing in the shade, while their brothers the pigeons line the telephone wires in radiant sunshine, waiting for their daily feed to spill forth from Mr. Johnson's sack of seed and cracked corn. Sunday morning, 10 a.m. High African clouds in the west, alamanda spilled in yellow spikes and coils across the fence. In the backyard: a neighbor's cat. At the sound of the opening window it flees, startled, then hesitates at the top of the wall to glance back—at what?—and as my eye tracks its gaze I catch a sudden motion in the overgrown grass, frantic circling too big for a lizard, too desperate, and even as I notice it and begin to speak, even as I call out *Hey, come see something strange in the yard* I realize, in that instant, what it must be—a bird, mauled, its weary struggle for survival— and wish I could unsay it, wish I could avert the gaze of my conscience because already I foresee the morning slipping away—a box, a warm towel, a bowl of water, and the calls to the Humane Society, and the drive to Fort Lauderdale to tender its fragile body to the Wild Animal Hospital, a shaded compound of blackbirds and parrots, box turtles and one-eared rabbits—and now Sam has come over to watch with me and I cannot will away the obvious, and he dashes out the back door to investigate, and now the day has been taken from us, seized, wrenched away, a day of rest I would covet even against that ring of blood and spilled feathers, the slender broken bones in the lawn, and now we are drawn into the circle of its small life, obligated by our witness, impossible to deny or retract, committed long before the dull slow course of a thought can be born into language, before the image is set into words, as Sam's words come to me now across the hot summer grass: *Dad, it's alive. A kind of bird. It's hurt. A dove.*

EL BALSERITO

Because my Spanish is chips-and-salsa simple, and I am desirous of improving upon it, and delighted whenever I can puzzle out on my own some new word or phrase, I am listening in on the conversation of the two Cuban men next to me at the counter of the plumbing supply store in Little Haiti, and when I hear the word *balserito* I recognize this to be a diminutive of *balsero*, "the rafter," that symbol of the Cuban-American experience, those cast ashore on scrapwood rafts emblematic of an entire community's exile, and when the one man goes out to his truck and comes back with a little plastic dashboard toy of Goofy and another Disney character floating in an inner tube, and the other man, laughing and smiling at the joke asks, *Quien es el otro?*, pointing at the smaller figure, I know that this is Max, Goofy's son, because we have just taken Sam to see *A Goofy Movie*, a story of father-son bonding in the cartoon universe, a universe in many ways more familiar to me than this one, though of course I say nothing to the men, not wanting to admit I have been eavesdropping, or betray my linguistic insufficiency, the degree to which I am an outsider here, in Miami, a place unlike any other I have known, a city we have fixed upon like Rust Belt refugees eager to buy a little piece of the sunshine, to mortgage a corner of the American Dream, where already Sam has begun to master the local customs, youngest and most flexible, first to make landfall, betraying the generational nature of acculturation the way the poems of my students at the state university do, caught between past and present worlds, transplanted parents looking back to Havana while the children are native grown, rooted to the soil, though the roots of *las palmas* are notoriously shallow, hence their propensity to topple in a hurricane, tropical storm, even the steady winter tradewind bearing its flotilla of makeshift sails across the Straits of Florida, so many this season that some mornings, jogging along the boardwalk in the shadow of the luxury hotels, I have come upon three rafts washed up in a single mile of beach, ragged planks and styrofoam and chicken-wire, filthy and abandoned but curiously empowered, endowed with a violent, residual energy, like shotgun casings in a field of corn stubble or the ruptured jelly of turtle eggs among mangroves, chrysalides discarded as the cost of the journey, shells of arrival, shells of departure.

SYLVIA PLATH

In truth I care little about your mother or your father, scars or bell jars, the suicidal hive, the husband against whom I am ignorantly prejudiced and willing to remain so. It is not the life but the poems that matter to me, those you abandoned with mere hints and allegations, Christmas toys agog on the rug, their hungry mouths, demanding as tulips, impatient as an infant. So they appear, sometimes, as glassy ornaments in a pitch-black elm tree eked from the seeds of predawn misery, the terror of isolation and mist from which they emerged, one a day, as with Van Gogh at Saint Remy, invoking the torment of root and marrow, touched by the sugar of abandonment, the prefiguration of the void, odor of gas, a new deep bruise, your magic moon in eclipse at last, stiff as a hard-bitten biscuit or British upper lip.

And then the leap, the pall of heaven, ruddy blood, an open oven.

1963. London.

This morning, painting the new bookshelves in the garage, white slabs ready for the wall's empty rack, I watched the sawn lumber rise up as plinths, as teeth in the mouth of one who calls me, as I too am summoned, in the hours before the dawn, by poems and by children.

It is not for your death but for your orphans that I love you.

They are as beautiful as ivory, as adamant as the chisel that carved them. I can see them stretched out before me in the fog like white stones, mile markers along a country road that ends, too suddenly, in the last ripe realization of the abyss.

Totem. Child. Paralytic. Gigolo. Mystic. Kindness. Words. Contusion. Balloons. Edge.

MANITOBA

Ten miles in we came upon the locusts, road striped and banded with them, fields plagued and shadowed with their mass, fulsome, darker than cloud-dapple, slick as shampoo beneath the wheels. In the next town we stopped to scrape them from the radiator with our pocket knives. Grasshoppers, their bodies crushed and mangled, scaled and armatured, primordial, pharoanic, an ancient horde of implacable charioteers, black ooze caking the headlights to blindness, mindless yellow legs still kicking. Not much in that town: sidewalks grown with goldenrod, grain elevator on the old railroad siding. Not much besides wheat and gasoline, the ragged beauty of the heat-painted prairie, wind with the texture of coiled rope, the solitude of the plains unrolling beyond limit of comprehension. It was time to hit the road. Charlie grabbed a root beer; I topped-up the oil. We hosed out the dead and drove on.

PLUMS

I'm sitting on a hill in Nebraska, in morning sunlight, looking out across the valley of the Platte River. My car is parked far below, in the lot behind the rest stop wigwam, beyond which runs the highway. Beyond the highway: stitch-marks of the railroad; the sandy channels and bars of the Platte, a slow wide bend of cottonwood saplings metallic in the sun; beyond the river a hazy, Cezanne-like geometry of earthy blues, greens, and browns fading, at last, into the distance. Barrel music rises up from the traffic on I-80, strings of long-haul truckers rolling west, rolling east, the great age of the automobile burning down before my eyes, a thing of colossal beauty and thoughtlessness. For lunch, in a paper bag: three ripe plums and a cold piece of chicken. It is not yet noon. My senses are alive to the warmth of the sun, the smell of the blood of the grass, the euphoria of the journey, the taste of fruit, fresh plums, succulent and juicy, especially the plums.

So much depends upon the image: chickens, asphodel, a numeral, a seashell;

one white peony flanged with crimson;

a chunk of black ore carried up from the heart of anthracite to be found by a child alongside the tracks like the token vestige of a former life—what is it? *coal*—a touchstone polished by age and handling, so familiar as to be a kind of fetish, a rabbit's foot worn down to bone, a talisman possessed of an entirely personal, associative, magical significance.

Why do I still carry it, that moment in Nebraska?

Was it the first time I'd been west, first time driving across the country? Was it the promise of open space, the joy of setting out, the unmistakable goodness of the land and the people, the first hint of connection with the deep wagon-ruts of the dream, the living tissue through which the valley of the Platte has channeled the Mormons and the 49ers, the Pawnee and the Union Pacific, this ribbon of highway beneath a sky alive with the smoke of our transit, the body of the past consumed by the engine of our perpetual restlessness? How am I to choose among these things? Who am I to speak for that younger vision of myself, atop a hill in Nebraska, bathed in morning light? I was there. I bore witness to that moment. I heard it pass, touched it, tasted its mysterious essence. I bear it with me even now, an amulet smooth as a fleshless fruit stone.

Plums.

I have stolen your image, William Carlos Williams. Forgive me. They were delicious, so sweet and so cold.

THE WRECK

Again on the highway with tears in my eyes, cadenced by rhythm of concrete and steel, music of cloud vapor, music of signs—Blue Flame Clown Rental/Color Wheel Fencing—again overcome, again fever-driven, transported among the pylons and skid marks of the inevitable, sirens and call boxes of a life I have laid claim to with a ticket found by chance in the pocket of a secondhand overcoat. And if it should come to that, if my fate is to be splayed on an altar of steel, heart held forth on an Aztec dagger of chrome, if this, then still I say it was beautiful, the freedom and speed with which you conveyed me, the way and the will, and I won't renounce the reek of acrid rubber or deny the need that sent me there, and I will not regret the purpose, the vehicle, the white line, the choice, and I will not mistake the message for the voice.

HARRYETTE MULLEN

Harryette Mullen is the author of five books of poetry,
including *Tree Tall Woman* (Energy Earth Communications,
1981), *Trimmings* (Tender Buttons Books, 1991) *S*PeRM*K*T*
(Singing Horse Press, 1992), *Muse and Drudge* (Singing Horse
Press, 1995) and *Sleeping With the Dictionary* (University of
California Press, 2002). Among her awards are a Dobie-
Paisano Fellowship from the Texas Institute of Letters, a grant
from the Wurlitzer Foundation, and a Gertrude Stein Award
for Innovative Writing. She is Associate Professor of English
and African American Studies at The University of California
at Los Angeles.

SOUVENIR FROM ANYWHERE

People of color untie-dyed. Got nothing to lose but your CPT-shirts. You're all just a box of crayons. The whole ball of wax would make a lovely decorator candle on a Day of the Dead Santeria Petro Vodou altar. Or how about these yin-yang earrings to balance your energy? This rainbow crystal necklace, so good for unblocking your chi and opening the chakras? Hey, you broke it, you bought it! No checks accepted. Unattended children will be sold as slaves.

Simultaneously
straightforward
yet so ambiguous...

Shifting between fun -
representing politics.

We know what
is right but
how does this
come into reality?

Art.

Be generous
with your reader.

ONCE EVER AFTER

There was this princess who wet the bed through many mattresses, she was so attuned. She neither conversed with magical beasts nor watched her mother turn into a stairwell or a stoop. Her lips were. Her hair was. Her complexion was. Her beauty or her just appearance. What she wore. She was born on a chessboard, with parents and siblings, all royal. Was there a witch? Was she enchanted, or drugged? When did she decide to sleep? Dreaming a knight in armor, she thought it meant jousting. His kind attack with streamers. A frog would croak. A heart would cough after only one bite. Something was red. There was wet and there was weather. She couldn't make it gold without his name. Her night shifts in the textile mill. She forgot she was a changeling peasant girl. Spinning, she got pricked. That's where roses fell and all but one fairy wept. It remains that she be buried alive, knowing that a kiss is smaller than a delayed hunger.

THE LUNAR LUTHERAN

In chapels of opals and spice, O Pisces pal, your social pep makes you a friend to all Episcopals. Brush off lint, gentile, but it's not intelligent to beshrew the faith of Hebrews. I heard this from a goy who taught yoga in the home of Goya. His Buddhist robe hid this budding D bust in this B movie dud. If Ryan bites a rep, a Presbyterian is best in prayer. Oh tears oxen trod! To catch oil, or a man born to the manor, you need a Catholic, Roman. On Mon. morn, Mom hums "Om" with no other man but Norm or Ron. A Morman son would gladly leave a gas slave in Las Vegas for a hut in Utah. These slums I'm from, I'm leaving, Miss Lum, with a slim sum donated by some Muslims. What would it cost to gain the soul of an agnostic? Where the atheist is at, God only knows! 'Tis hate, he is at the heist. A Baptist was able to stab a pit bull when the sun hid behind some Hindus. To fan a mess, I write manifestos. So said the lunar Lutheran.

FREE RADICALS

She brought the radish for the horses, but not a bouquet for Mother's Day. She brought the salad to order with an unleavened joke. Let us dive in and turn up green in search of our roots. She sang the union maid with a lefty longshoreman. They all sang rusty freedom songs, once so many tongues were loosened. She went to bed sober as always, without a drop of wine. She was invited to judge a spectacle. They were a prickly pair in a restaurant of two-way mirrors with rooms for interrogation. The waiter who brought a naming dessert turned the heat from bickering to banter. She braked for jerk chicken on her way to meet the patron saint of liposuction. His face was cut from the sunflower scene, as he was stuffing it with cheesecake. Meanwhile, she slurped her soup alone at the counter before the gig. Browsers can picture his uncensored bagel rolling around in cyberspace. His half-baked metaphor with her scrambled ego. They make examples of intellectuals who don't appreciate property. She can't just trash the family-style menu or order by icon. Now she's making *kimchee* for the museum that preserved her history in a jar of pickled pig feet. They'd fix her oral tradition or she'd trade her oral fixation. Geechees are rice eaters. It's good to get a rice cooker if you cook a lot of rice. Please steam these shellfish at your own risk. Your mother eats blue-green algae to rid the body of free radicals.

DIM LADY

My honeybunch's peepers are nothing like neon. Today's special at Red Lobster is redder than her kisser. If Liquid Paper is white, her racks are institutional beige. If her mop were Slinkys, dishwater Slinkys would grow on her noggin. I have seen table-cloths in Shakey's Pizza Parlors, red and white, but no such picnic colors do I see in her mug. And in some minty-fresh mouthwashes there is more sweetness than in the garlic breeze my main squeeze wheezes. I love to hear her rap, yet I'm aware that Muzak has a hipper beat. I don't know any Marilyn Monroes. My ball and chain is plain from head to toe. And yet, by gosh, my scrumptious Twinkie has as much sex appeal for me as any lanky model or platinum movie idol who's hyped beyond belief.

NAKED STATUES

Oscars for the war of noses. With a mummy out of Egypt, a prosthetic muppet. Opening shot: cliche of travel genre. In several scenes, a woman put together in black, white, or khaki. A woman with her back up like his map of mountain. Finally, she dies. Then, at last, he dies. So romantic are the patient English. This all went on when I was making up my syllabus. Telephone and radio told who the winners were. I didn't need a crystal. Last time I watched was leopard chair and whoopie cushion. That's when I saw the industry of light, our buttered roll. These are the friends of inklish, I was told, by someone from an anglophile race. They read all the great books and perform them in the garden of naked statues.

THE ANTHROPIC PRINCIPLE

The pope of cosmology addresses a convention. When he talks the whole atmosphere changes. He speaks through a computer. When he asks can you hear me, the whole audience says yes. It's a science locked up in a philosophical debate. There are a few different theories. There could be many different realities. You might say ours exists because we do. You could take a few pounds of matter, heat it to an ungodly temperature, or the universe was a freak accident. There may be a limit to our arrogance, but one day the laws of physics will read like a detailed instruction manual. A plane that took off from its hub in my hometown just crashed in the President's hometown. The news anchor says the pilot is among the dead. I was hoping for news of the President's foreign affair with a diplomat's wife. I felt a mystical connection to the number of confirmed dead whose names were not released. Like the time I was three handshakes from the President. Like when I thought I heard that humanitarians dropped a smart blond on the Chinese embassy. Like when the cable was severed and chairs fell from the sky because the pilot flew with rusty maps. What sane pilot would land in that severe rain with hard hail and gale-force wind. With no signal of distress. With no foghorns to warn the civilians, the pilot lost our moral compass in the bloody quagmire of collateral damage. One theory says it's just a freak accident locked up in a philosophical debate. It's like playing poker and all the cards are wild. Like the arcane analysis of a black box full of insinuations of error.

DENIGRATION

Did we surprise our teachers who had niggling doubts about the picayune brains of small black children who reminded them of clean pickaninnies on a box of laundry soap? How muddy is the Mississippi compared to the third-longest river of the darkest continent? In the land of the Ibo, the Hausa, and the Yoruba, what is the price per barrel of nigrescence? Though slaves, who were wealth, survived on niggardly provisions, should inheritors of wealth fault the poor enigma for lacking a dictionary? Does the mayor demand a recount of every bullet or does city hall simply neglect the black alderman's district? If I disagree with your beliefs, do you chalk it up to my negligible powers of discrimination, supposing I'm just trifling and not worth considering? Does my niggling concern with trivial matters negate my ability to negotiate in good faith? Though Maroons, who were unruly Africans, not loose horses or lazy sailors, were called renegades in Spanish, will I turn any blacker if I renege on this deal?

COALS TO NEWCASTLE, PANAMA HATS FROM ECUADOR

Watching television in Los Angeles. This scene performed in real time. In real life, a pretty picture walking and sitting still. It's still life with fried spam, lite poundcake, nondairy creme. It's death by chocolate. It's corporate warfare as we know it. I'm stuck on the fourth step. There's no statue or stature of limitations. I'll be emotionally disturbed for as long as it takes. You can give a man a rock or you can teach him to rock. Access your higher power. Fax back the map of your spiritual path. Take twenty drops tincture of worry wort. Who's paying for this if you're not covered? You're too simple to be so difficult. Malicious postmodernism. Petroleum jelly donut dunked in elbow grease. You look better going than coming. You look like death eating microwave popcorn. Now that I live alone, I'm much less introspective. Now you sound more like yourself.

BLACK NIKES

We need quarters like King Tut needed a boat. A slave could row him to heaven from his crypt in Egypt full of loot. We've lived quietly among the stars, knowing money isn't what matters. We only bring enough to tip the shuttle driver when we hitch a ride aboard a trailblazer of light. This comet could scour the planet. Make it sparkle like a fresh toilet swirling with blue. Or only come close enough to brush a few lost souls. Time is rotting as our bodies wait for now I lay me down to earth. Noiseless patient spiders paid with dirt when what we want is stardust. If nature abhors an expensive appliance, why does the planet suck ozone? This is a big-ticket item, a thickety ride. Please page our home and visit our sigh on the wide world's ebb. Just point and cluck at our new persuasion shoes. We're opening the gate that opens our containers for recycling. Time to throw down and take off on our launch. This flight will nail our proof of pudding. The thrill of victory is, we're exiting earth. We're leaving all this dirt.

NAOMI SHIHAB NYE

Naomi Shihab Nye is the author of seven poetry collections, including *Red Suitcase* (1994) and *Fuel* (1998), both from BOA Editions. Her award-winning books for young readers include *What Have You Lost* (1999) and *Come With Me: Poems for a Journey* (2000), both from Harper Collins. Her book of prose poems is *Mint Snowball* (Anhinga Press, 2001). She has received a Guggenheim Fellowship, two Jane Addams Children's Book Awards and the Witter Bynner Fellowship from the Library of Congress. She is featured in the documentary, *The Language of Life with Bill Moyers,* and lives in San Antonio, Texas.

I WAS THINKING OF POEMS

In the fields our eyes whirled inside a blur of green. Before I wore glasses I came here. Thought the world was soft at the far edges for real. Green rim of trees alongside anyone's life. Stalk. Pod. Tendril. Blossom. On a farm you had time. Your mind on words. Turned over gently and longly inside your head. Damp dirt under dry surface.

He said "Rain" or "Easy." Said "String" or "Yellow." A boy said "Yes sir" but meant "I don't get it." A phrase dangled. Strip of cloud. Wide angle. Line breaks. Where the asparagus row turned into the beets.

THE MIND OF SQUASH

Overnight, and quietly. Beneath the scratchy leaf we thicken and expand so fast you can't believe. Sun pours into us. We drink midnight too, blue locust lullaby feeding our graceful sleep. When you come back, we are fat. Doubled in the dark. Faster than you are. Sometimes we grow together, two of us twining out from the same stalk, conversational blossoms. Bring the bucket. Bring the small knife with the sharp blade. Bring the wind to cool our wide span of leaves, each one bigger than a human head, bigger than dinner plates. Wait till you find the giant prize we have hidden from you all along—no muscle-rich upper arm exceeds its size. But the farmer doesn't like it. Too big for selling, he says. Only for zucchini bread. Never mind. We like it. We have our own pride.

LIVING ALONE INSIDE ONE'S OWN BODY

Some days light falls in warm sheets. The metallic gray sky seems reflective—I know that weather. Fear takes on a familiar taste. Even regret, that stone, that peach pit turned on the tongue. And the man raking next door before dawn— how can he see what he is raking? I like the sound of bricks being stacked, the heavy clink. I like the dragging grate of his rake's teeth through wet, dark leaves.

BRIGHT NEEDLE POKED THROUGH DARK CLOTH

Light arriving in villages, lifting stone, opening shadows, a girl finds a circle of light on her hand. Even the broom in its corner, soles of shoes jumbled on the doorstep, a book left open till it blinks inside a film of dust—without morning did not belong to one another. Did not remember how they were invented or touched.

PARIS

Once my father and I were flying home from the Middle East and we stopped in Paris for 24 hours. Our taxi driver told us what happiness was. "It's when you don't want anything. You don't hate it, you just don't want it. You like it, in fact. You just don't want it." I told him he sounded like a Buddhist, but he didn't want that either. He said nobody in Paris was happy. He let us off on a street where vendors sold cream puffs and hosiery and snazzy yellow-toed shoes and pears and fresh baguettes and wine. The whole day and night I was in Paris, I bought nothing. Not one thing. Not even a postcard. At the restaurant I asked the waitress to choose for me, partly because I couldn't read French, but also because I wasn't sure what I wanted. We could have changed our tickets and stayed 10 days. My father wanted to. I could have bought Parisian socks, a tin of lemon drops. My father kept shaking his head, asking, "What's the rush?" He told me I'd be sorry later. It wasn't the first time he'd predicted this. But I felt happy in Paris, so briefly, breezing up and down those streets I'd never know with my empty hands.

MINT SNOWBALL II

I passed through Shelbyville, Illinois a few days ago for the first time in 35 years, the town where my great-grandfather had his drugstore and made his mint snowballs. I walked up and down the main street, happy the town seemed to be thriving—no boards over shop windows. Upbeat, old-fashioned, lovely. I went to my great-grandparent's old house and talked to the man who lives there now. Within three minutes of my arrival, he said, "You know what I will never forget in my whole life?" (He is 70) "The taste of that mint snowball your great-grandfather used to make."

I almost fainted on the grass... "And how old were you when you had it?" He said, "Between the ages of five and ten—my mom used to get it for me when I was good."

HIS LIFE

I don't know what he thinks about. At night the vault of his face closes up. He could be underground. He could be buried treasure. He could be a donkey trapped in the Bisbee Mine, lowered in so long ago with pulleys and belts, kicking, till its soft fur faded and eyes went blind. They made donkeys pull the little carts of ore from seam to seam. At night, when the last men stepped into the creaking lift, the donkeys cried. Some lived as long as 17 years down there. The miners still feel bad about it. They would have hauled them out to breathe real air in the evenings, but the chute was so deep and they'd never be able to force them in again.

RAIN FALLING INTO THE RIVER—THAT MOMENT AS THEY MERGE

In a cottage by a river, a man made stories. He lived so fully in his room it was hard to get him out. His room grew jungles, revising itself with light. I think he would stand in his room staring out at rain falling into the river and wonder why people went anywhere to begin with—this world of avenues fashioning, tugging, offering what we learn to need—he could see the sadness in that without even entering it. Whole catalogues of sadness—species, radiant wings, and eyes. He chose his quiet kind and planted banana leaf palms. He drew little men who turn into donkeys. Little girls who fly into flowers and sleep there. When people invited him to come and talk to them about being an artist, he declined. It was hard to talk to more than one person at a time, to say the right words to enter so many ears at once. Better the river's quiet pulse, the heaping mountains of cloud gathering silently on any horizon, tilting the day a different way. He drew a little boy and girl who wanted to be grown-up until bedtime came—then they were ready to be small again. Sometimes when I can't sleep I think of his pen in the room next to the river, shaping, shaping, a jeweled crown, a kangaroo, a billowing tree. Since he died he's rewritten the whole neighborhood.

WORKING FOR TOM

Again the truck labeled "TOM'S PEANUTS" swoops past at a corner and I lean forward jealously to see the driver's face. Across the city silver machines wait to be filled with peanuts, candies, gums. When the truck empties, that driver gets to go home, or loads another truck, but I cannot imagine him always wandering, dreaming peanuts and peanut butters, George Washington Carver's infinite variations. While I, in my small house under the trees, seem to stay on the job all day and night, sharpening pencils, wadding envelopes, clocking the hours by occasional squirrel feet scrabbling across the roof. Even while dreaming, I make a list of things to do, words to contemplate: *radiant, stealth, help!* But the world is eating peanuts. The world is happy with its simple life.

ISLAND

All the envelopes on the desk are bleaching quietly, swallowing their own addresses, forgetting where they came from. At night they fly out the windows, circle the house and scoot back in through the louvres. That's why they're lying in a pile when we wake up. It's hard to remember the big land connected to other land. It's hard to remember who wrote this, if anyone answered. See that little sail way off by the line where sea and sky get together? It's a letter. It's to all of us. That's the happiest line in the world.

CHARLES SIMIC

Charles Simic was awarded The Pulitzer Prize for a collection of prose poems, *The World Doesn't End* (Harcourt Brace, 1989). He is the author of over two dozen books, including *Hotel Insomnia* (1992), *A Wedding in Hell* (1994), *Walking the Black Cat* (1996), *Jackstraws* (1999), and *Night Picnic* (2001), all published by Harcourt Brace. His essays and memoirs are gathered in five books, including *A Fly in the Soup* (University of Michigan Press, 2001). Among his other awards are The Harriet Monroe Poetry Award, a Guggenheim Fellowship, a MacArthur Foundation Fellowship, and awards from The National Institute of Arts and Letters and The American Academy of Arts and Letters. He has taught for more than twenty-five years at the University of New Hampshire in Durham.

I was stolen by the gypsies. My parents stole me right back. Then the gypsies stole me again. This went on for some time. One minute I was in the caravan suckling the dark teat of my new mother, the next I sat at the long dining room table eating my breakfast with a silver spoon.

It was the first day of spring. One of my fathers was singing in the bathtub; the other one was painting a live sparrow the colors of a tropical bird.

TERRA INCOGNITA

America still waits to be discovered. Its tramps and poets resemble early navigators setting out on journeys of exploration. Even in its cities there are still places left blank by the map makers.

This afternoon it's a movie house, which, for some reason, is showing two black-and-white horror films. In them the night is always falling. Someone is all alone someplace they shouldn't be. If there's a house, it must be the only one for miles around. If there's a road, it must be deserted. The trees are bare, or if they have leaves, they rustle darkly. The sky still has a little gray light. It is the kind of light in which even one's own hands appear unfamiliar, a stranger's hands.

On the street again, the man in a white suit turning the comer could be the ghost of the dead poet Frank O'Hara.

OLD POSTCARD OF 42ND STREET AT NIGHT

I'm looking for the mechanical chess player with a red turban. I hear Pythagoras is there queuing up, and Monsieur Pascal, who hears the silence inside God's ear.

Eternity and time are the coins it requires, everybody's portion of it, for a quick glimpse of that everything which is nothing.

Night of the homeless, the sleepless, night of those winding the watches of their souls, the stopped watches, before the machine with mirrors.

Here's a raised hand covered with dime-store jewels, a hand like "a five-headed Cerberus," and two eyes opened wide in astonishment.

Are Russian cannibals worse than the English? Of course. The English eat only the feet, the Russians the soul. "The soul is a mirage," I told Anna Alexandrovna, but she went on eating mine anyway.

"Like a superb confit of duck, or like a sparkling littleneck clam still in its native brine?" I inquired. But she just rubbed her belly and smiled at me from across the table.

Time—the lizard in the sunlight. It doesn't move, but its eyes are wide open. *They love to gaze into our faces and hearken to our discourse.*

It's because the very first men were lizards. If you don't believe me, go grab one by the tail and see it come right off.

My guardian angel is afraid of the dark. He pretends he's not, sends me ahead, tells me he'll be along in a moment. Pretty soon I can't see a thing. "This must be the darkest corner of heaven," someone whispers behind my back. It turns out her guardian angel is missing too. "It's an outrage," I tell her. "The dirty little cowards leaving us all alone," she whispers. And of course, for all we know, I might be a hundred years old already, and she just a sleepy little girl with glasses.

THE MAGIC STUDY OF HAPPINESS

In the smallest theater in the world the bread crumbs speak. It's a mystery play on the subject of a lost paradise. Once there was a kitchen with a table on which a few crumbs were left. Through the window you could see your young mother by the fence talking to a neighbor. She was cold and kept hugging her thin dress tighter and tighter. The clouds in the sky sailed on as she threw her head back to laugh.

Where the words can't go any further—there's the hard table. The crumbs are watching you as you in turn watch them. The unknown in you and the unknown in them attract each other. The two unknowns are like illicit lovers when they're exceedingly and unaccountably happy.

Lover of endless disappointments with your collection of old postcards, I'm coming! I'm coming! You want to show me a train station with its clock stopped at five past five. We can't see inside the station master's window because of the grime. We don't even know if there's a train waiting on the platform, much less if a woman in black is hurrying through the front door. There are no other people in sight, so it must be a quiet station. Some small town so effaced by time it has only one veiled widow left, and now she too is leaving with her secret.

THE OLD MAN TOLD ME

There was a movie theater here once. It played silent films. It was like watching the world through dark glasses on a rainy evening.

One night the piano player mysteriously disappeared. We were left with the storming sea that made no sound, and a beautiful woman on a long, empty beach whose tears rolled down silently as she watched me falling asleep in my mother's arms.

OUR ANGELIC ANCESTOR

Rimbaud should have gone to America instead of Lake Chad. He'd be a hundred years old and rummaging through a discount store. Didn't he say he liked stupid paintings, signs, popular engravings, erotic books with bad spelling, novels of our grandmothers?

Arthur, poor boy, you would have walked the length of Fourteenth Street and written many more "Illuminations."

Poetry: three mismatched shoes at the entrance of a dark alley.

KAREN VOLKMAN

Karen Volkman's first book, *Crash's Law* (W.W. Norton, 1998),
was chosen for The National Poetry Series. Her second book,
Spar (University of Iowa Press, 2002), received The Iowa
Poetry Prize. Her poems have appeared in the *Paris Review*,
New Republic, Colorado Review, Fence, and other journals. She
is Poet-in-Residence at The University of Chicago.

And when the nights, the May nights, the moan nights, when they come. When they come, the wrong words will follow, glancing sorrow. My idiot Spring, with its hot heart and figures, the flowers lame laws in a weatherbane wind. Where is my silver harrow, my ore-waif strewing pierce-bits with every skip? (In one story, she plays the accordion on the Traumplatz, a tune, a veiny tune, that wouldn't please a monkey.) Where is my inkblot midnight, full of eyes? Yawn, I would say, gall-mouth, fertile fallow: a driblet, a teacup, a chalice, a reeking wave.

And when the morning, the bruise morning, the brine morning, when it *thens*—cracked alphabet of revelation—stitch and line—*then* the foot marries the forward, the fall the toward. Then the null and the next are cousins, in high-noon hammocks of incestuous list. Then what should I do with my waver, my very war, my sky-blue exigency, bloody with minutes? Which extremest west will swallow all this tending?

I never wish to sing again as I used to, when two new eyes could always stain the sea, of tangent worlds, indolent as callows, and the clock went backward for a skip, to rise, to set.

Some will twine grass to fit in a thimble, some will carve bread to mend a craggy wall, some in the slantest midnight cry for sleep. When the pitch-owl swallows the moon, what welt will show it? Sighing helps nothing, raspberries raw and green, in the form of a heart

imperfectly divided. A wave grows sharper close to the shore. Some own words like strips of scape and summon. It is possible to suffer even in the sun. And race the steep noon to its highest, hoary gate. Stares drop under the sky; silence of a windslap; and a scar drifts out of air to stand whistling:

She who listens poorly will always be calling. She who sounds silence drowns with the dumb.

She who cuts her hands off must drink with her tongue.

I was watching for it, everytime watching, for the neck that was bent, for the nape that was bare. The hand holding a cup was holding a thin cup, then the cup was broken, and the fluid gone. So things were the same—eyes stayed blue, limbs retained their curves, slacks and sleeves. Someplace more thoughtless something would happen, less full of couches and women and legs. The windows were waiting, and the lamps, and the hat donned once, discarded, and the hesitant hips, and the whisper which forebore. For all was intent, potential, not fulfill.

I go out sometimes, like a shadowless ghost, less remnant than lip, in the incomparable midnight of intransigent mist, and the doomsayers and lockpickers, cloud-like in clairvoyance. Lad, you keep the latch hanging, keep the curtain drawn. Beyond blue night, when the puppets are sleeping, the stars all coiled in their tremulous wheel, the thin moon summers in my goldenest gaze, awakening dreaming oceans, to drown, to roam.

Sky-eyed scholar, pale Confucius: Put down your book.

If it be event, I go towards and not back. I go tower, not floor. I listen but rarely learn, I take into account occasionally, but more often there are lips to kiss, words to pass from tongue to mouth, white entire. It knows a few names about what I am, it goes door to door saying *She* is or *Her ire*. But when the rainbows are handles I hold dragging earth to more vivid disasters, oh swinging by the strap. You thought she was a dimwit flapper, really she's a chemist with a taste for distress. You thought she came with guarantees, really she's your nightmare hatcheck has a vagrant head. I sort of sometimes go by the book, the need to move being visage, mask you wear like dark sky or water (water that boils or breaks or scares the flame). We don't need a nest to grow in, a bed to sleep. In the clairvoyance of loving wrongly, o glass pillow o swallow, is dream is dare is dagger. Your turn.

There comes a time to rusticate the numbers. The way the birds, jug jug, mount in steepleless processions, or the barely comprehensible division of our hands. Or the cliff with the face of a galled god, appalling. And these are boundable, we count them, each and each.

But my zero, windy and sleepless, how to teach it? It speaks to the rain, the spare precipitation—it says, Desert conditions, but I fathom the sea—and rain in its meticulous sermon mumbles back. Talk, talk, in shrill slaps, in strident speculations. As the almond trees flash the gold, precocious blossoms our cold maids call blind psyche. And this was me. I give you my digital, my radial, my baldest baby. While annul! cries the fitful keeper, who sears and scalds. But my zero, sum and province, whole howl, skies the all.

Although the paths lead into the forest, we are bitter with the bodies of days that end too early. All things tend to a darker dissolution. In a pond, the green flecks adrift, the ducks are dimming, murk preserving rust brine and the fish with a marl fin. We may be guided by grieved grass, the workless, mossy flesh, which tufts the dumb stones in their staunch sleep, awake.

Women who tend the brown days can only listen, it is this that quivers—the no-time, the nothing—which birds have swallowed like lucid beads of sight. If you dig in the earth with your fingers, with your stick, what to do with the blameless accruings? You strike lack. You slap the long oblivion of a blank alive with harm. If it is morning, why are we dying? There used to be so many stories we could sing, the tongue of luck, the dreamwork. And how the days fall like random raindrops, and leave no stain, beside the quiet streams where time is seeping, bone, blame.

What we know is too full of tremors. An ague takes me like a blade, glancing to futures not mappable as landscape. And you, whom I give my most infinite existence—the dream of a hand and its attendant caress—for this we are quiet, for this we veil our eyes.

Which things will fulfill us? Time's tokens leave their lesions, night and rumor. Ecstasy, to be remembered. A coil of heartbreak in a handshake, a certain sigh. So far, kept hemmed in the instant, of tinny mallets and amnesiac keys—mystic music, love's longing and longing's lees.

Mere predator, do no more leaving. The child bit on the throat will always sing palely, melody sweetened by starlight and dim with harm. It is to *be won* that we wager. Drink the dark dram, lover, and be wine.

Shrewd star, who crudes our naming: you should be flame. Should be everyone's makeshift measure, rife with tending—constellations called *Scatter* or *Spent Memory* or *Crown of Yes* or *Three Maids Slow in Pleasure.* Some days my eyes are green like verdigris, or green like verdant ardor, or like impair. Does it matter the law is a frame to hang your heart in? This *was.* I saw it, schemed it, bled it. I was *then.* Or: I ran with all my leagues of forgotten steps to reach you. A rose said to a rumor, is fame what blooms with flanged petals, or is that cause? Are blind bones brighter in skulled winter or spring-a-dazing? I am asking the most edgeless questions, so words will keep them, so the green gods in my mind will lull and lie. But constellation *Mute Cyclops,* my ravaged child, weeps every eye.

I have a friend. My friend is a sky. There are dark, starved places that do nothing but blur and spend, and the quick sharp blue-black lightning streaks called *punish*. If you wish to do what is known only as "to rest," " to sleep," " to live," you and my friend will have *nothing* to speak of.

He says. Girls fall through holes, occasionally on purpose. He says, Many shapes of web make the rope that will stay you. He says, A bitter metal forms the bit that slits your tongue.

When they ask, What is your friend, that you ash and azure for him? I sing boxless wind in a blanched meadow, scree and scrawl. It is *not* because doors keep the light out, or doom is mortal. It is *not* because dawn calls weather, wander, weigh. If words are wire and can whip him, *this is* the scar.

I won't go in today, I'll stay out today. I won't go home today, instead I'll go to sea. Today is a lot of work, yesterday wiser. Yesterday is a path made out of feet, today is a screwball alarmclock with a mawkish tick. Today offends everyone with nebulous gesture: "I think." "Yes but." "Still really." "Gee well." This becomes language you know becomes destiny, still you know that operator listening in on the phone? She of the darker stare and windy grimace? Yes she is writing every word, I wouldn't leave that blur too conspicuous, knapsack of roar. I wouldn't give just anyone access, but you know best. Seems to me you go out a little too spryly, hardly a step really more of a *sprawl*. You packed your bags reasonably enough, but what about all that dubious baggage from last fall? Seems we're in for shriller weather, your eye no more mild decries tornado and scar. Today needs a few more devotees lacking grace. But yesterday, imperious echo, knows who you are.

LIZ WALDNER

Liz Waldner received The Iowa Poetry Prize for *A Point Is That Which Has No Part* (University of Iowa Press, 2000). Her other books of poetry include *Self and Simulacra* (Alice James Books, 2001) which received The Hawley Prize, *Etym(bi)ology* (Omnidawn Publishing, 2002) and *Dark Would: The Missing Person* (2002), a University of Georgia Press Contemporary Poetry Series winner. She lives in Seattle, Washington.

WEDNESDAY MORNING PRAY TIME

Trial. Tribulation. Psycho-sexual amputation. So busy. So big. What is happening here? O lord god in heaven save me from an uninhabitable moment. No eye contact feels safer in here. She has a bagel in her pocket. How come it's not bagle like bugle? The music of bugles is bagel-like, going round and round and coming out here. How can she but giggle at the French horn's effluence, etc. Also in evidence today that other hole in the psyche's ozone, figure of the Great Naught, Aquinas-esque estimation of the female sex as sewer, wound, Freudian source of the river of envy, poor yoni. All this, the road not taken today. Have I ignored it and has it gone away? No no row row boat, river, slipstream, ocean view, harbor home, harvest home, food bank, turkey dinner, table laden, linden the tree, linden the tea, the leap from forest canopy to golden savannah, Susanna don't you cry for me, for I've gone to Tanganyika with a thumb piano on my knee. Little Jack Horner, his corner. Thumb, plum, sex in a nutshell, plumb line, heart line, throw out the live line (phone sex) I mean lifeline, Jesus is coming for me. When he washed oh when he washed when my Jesus washed he washed my sins away. O happy day with thunder clouds, O dunderhead, O Donner, O Blitzen, all alone (a sorry pass) in the wrack of the roof of history, o tool Machiavellian, o fool antediluvian, o water well blessed, o accountant overdressed, o men, a men, women, and linen, a linnet and back to a linden, a tree (the voice says find a place to stop, stop, second hand channeling still the discourse on the watch, *the sad and happy clocks,* the pattern on his socks but actually, ouch, the big hand stopped with the tree). Bated breath on the hook of the line of communication dropped down from the otherwise empty heaven: in the beginning was the word and with it, heaven saved me.

DIS/*COEURS* ON THE METHOD

An awful lot of things are busy. A spider egg thing is throttled by the breeze and the spider bite on my wrist vein swells and makes a tiny golden seed. I am not sure what the bumblebees mean, dragging their shadows over the barn wall's computer screen. I live in the barn, and behind the blind of the bathroom window, the buzz can be sudden and too near for outside. As with words, a lot of the outside is inside in there.

What was yard hasn't been mown in months. Tall grasses move the way I crave to move with you through the no thing sex makes. There is also how the breeze feels in my sick ear and how the light goes through the maple noses here. Wasps sail trailing their legs behind like cripples with wings and find a wall and fly right in. The sun sears the windshield, shifts and slits sharp so fits of dark light bum into my brain.

What really can come in? The light is an electrochemical twitch, rod and cone, radio retina: *Come in, home.* The catbird call and the chainsaw whine flutter some drum. A wave moves through the inner ear sea and the sounds of the things of this world come to be. The doves inside the sand dollar are a skeletal olive branch the ocean offers me. The spider spit in my wrist, the grit in the oyster fruit, seed and flower at once. Goethe's analysis of the parts of plants: this becomes this becomes this: the thought of the body a figure of speech: "I want" one way to say the grass, the spider biting, my busyness. Some others, but not the heart.

HOUSEWIFE'S LAMENT

Here I am. Sam I am. Not Spam. Nor Pam, an awful name for another awful product. Blame. Lame. Negativity abounds. He'll say PMS makes the rounds. I do feel mean as a snake skinned. Once I was finned; before it did it, it looked me in the eye. It, the fish. Wife, wish. A kiss, a load of laundry, the washer in the faucet, the hinge in the wrist, the watcher in the clock face, impermanent wave tryst. Improbable. Bubble. Scheme burst. Scene 2, in which Artaud is advised he wears his volume oh so loud. Turn down that damn heart off. With a bristle bristle here and a bristle bristle there = our masculine ego has suffered some more. Repeat after me, I am a bore. Copy this 500 times. Nobody heard of carpal tunnel syndrome In Those Days. In the days of the bee sips from the leaf tip, the scent of minted air. Meanwhile, somewhere, etc. The relative humidity is 90 percent, the temperature 92. (One must never say temp, it is disgusting, like Pam.) Large statistics are in my brain. I don't even want your goddam kiss, mister plumber. Let's see if you have the sense to keep on walking. No, it appears you do not, which is a pity. You have no kind of humility. Except I bet with your mother but that's hardly relative. It's always the Me Show with you, or is that me? It's that volume knob again, transposes the brain waves of even the lowliest of reptiles, I gotta tell you and you, for all your racket, aren't going to be able to hear. Big sigh and irritations. If only I owned my own home.

A VERY BIG WIND

I dreamed a tornado. White-glove affair (no dust, no muss, *ich muss*, ichthys, fly fish, Icarus: look, pa, no hands nor flies on me) interrupted by this spinny missive from the heavens. National Weather Service mythology: Gods' messenger, Iris, spreads wings, lifts weights: isobars at god's gym with her homeys, The Fates. "Gymnopedies," metronome, music of now eerie spheres, "spears" is how you say that in Mississippi, where Zeus, ever handy with a caduceus, pierces the skies with his thunderbolts, screws up a few things, sends us a slinky of wind to tuck us in, or tuck into us, as the case may be—in any case, once again, a very big wind. And the fish rises to the flicked fly: alas, poor Icarus, he flew so well. The thunder rumbles across the river in, yep, the Catskills. Washington Irving or Julius, bowling balls or basket, beltway or Orion's belt, in a democracy we choose our heavens and our dearths, too, thereby. And here I set (not a hen, just southern), watching the trees' green ravishing, the wind moving them like you move me although I mostly only yearn to show my name means tree. Limbs long enough, eh?—but boned, excuse the expression. They, trees, meanwhile chant those names the druids knew before they became a major league team—and demonstrate that what the bird flew through is theirs, too: anything that moves you is, and helps you know your name. What does the tongue of tornado seek as licking, licking, this way it comes? More, more. Knowledge of houses, sex with the trees. The fish rises to the flicked fly's and yours to my need.

ADAM AU VERSO

He is holding his chin in a thoughtful way while he sleeps. It is a good thing he is not a pipe smoker; the pose would be too much. Birds are whistling up the hot day to come through the window for my left ear. I let him be thinking about these. "About" spatially, all about, like seeds scattered about the thistle and the mind a finch. No. Like clouds close about the treeline and the few checkmarks of swallows speckling the sky. More so. Thought the pebble, widening rings of water into feeling, the peculiar circular melancholy of the downward spiraling song of that bird I first heard in the woods in the middle of Peak's Island, Maine, that you go through to get from the ferry side which is the city side to the other, craggy ocean side. I lived there alone, Maine. I decided to call it a thrush, a word full enough in the throat to matter. Matter, a transitive and intransitive word. Thrush, throat, hoof and mouth, the toenails of strangers. Bleh. There are horribles, yes. There are also the songlines the thoughts travel, singing the world up out of its sleep, "its", the mind's, too, mine. Opals, eyes with cataracts and glimmers, mother of pearl excited to brilliance—his eyes flutter and almost open and I smile, it is so like a cartoon. In the beginning was life and then Looney Tunes, only in 1964 I didn't know it came in that order, I was being raised up as a vegetable, the sun grabbed my petals and pulled, I had nothing to do with it, I thought that that cartoon music while a pig shoots a rabbit and the sun has little arms coming out of its face near its ears that it rubs its eyes with were without reference and, so, everything. And not funny. I had no reference. Nor had god. But thirty years later, his eyelids flutter. He rubs his eyes with both fists and the world begins. I imagine I could have been a child, I imagine his mother upstairs was mine. Am I making another cartoon? A songline is drawn: one brow twitches, an especially quickening sparrow sings. Matters: the sleeper's elbow and knee almost meet. Out the window, the dead neighbor's lawn burro stands, confronting a little dead bush. But I must keep my eye on the sleeper who narrates with gesture and breath the world he lets be made from his sleep. A pale blue sheet covers his ribs.

REPRESENTATION

In a bedroom, in any bedroom, in a white room with white curtains, say, on each side of its window like bookends, like bouncers, like the angels with flaming swords at Eden, sit two guys playing guitars. Two guitars. Four women sit in four straight-backed chairs in front of two men with two guitars; that is, they sit facing the window. The curtains billow. The music billows. Notes flutter about the room like moths with no particular star in mind. On the women's faces, the blinds are down. Their worries line them like blinds, like staves. There, occasional notes from one or the other of the two guitars leave a trace like dust from a moth's wing—faint but distinguishable notation. In this way, the women note their songs. In this way, the women compose they faces. In this way, in any bedroom, facing anywhere, everything may be said to depend on who's *their,* *whose* their, who's there.

GUSTATORY/HORTATORY

Fine Dining, I thought, complete with capital letters. It is 8:06 in the morning, not the hour to think of fine dining, one would think, not the time to find it in one's mind like a strange hat found on one's kitchen chair at 3:27 in the afternoon, goodness, exclamatory, whence—and yet petted on the head and given a place at the table because found there. Oh the head of the table, the last supper, M. Prevert, prix fixe, meal prepared; to be dished and dissed, a plate like a halo behind yr head, soon to be hors d'oeuvre for the faithful even as behind your back the project progresses: make mincemeat out of, and hence back to dining, if not fine. Finely chopped, but the stuff in jars always looks like bruises. Not so fine. Fines for littering, fines for loitering, fines for beating your wife to a pulp (OJ). Mighty fine shine on ten silver pieces, a shekel, a bushel, sorghum, spelt, wheat. Wheat I thought, like so. 8:13 a.m., ante meridian, Latin on the tongue every day and who notes it? The placebo effect: I place the wafer on your tongue, my meaning in your mouth, we mostly think we know what one another is talking about. We are mostly wrong. Two people cannot eat the same food, held up as a profound thought. Personally, I do not find this lonely or even particularly true, since what does a baby at the breast do but eat, eventually, what you do? Or, whenever you like, eat a leaf of lettuce and eat light of days it ate. Shine Dining. This light on the sheet, that on bare foot, this other that makes the numbers 8 and 1 and 6; this that moves me to pen before breakfast, and that bidding, don't think capital P, just put it down and eat.

SUN DIAL

Call him up! Call him up! Jesus is on the line.

There in a bed, they are. One supposes that the other doesn't notice they're not supposed to be; however, she does more than notice. She feels what she sees. I speak here of me, who is not a girl in a T-shirt with flappy hair heading for her car over there without a coat. It's cold here where there's sun after so many days of grey to rain that doesn't always come. Words, neither. Maybe it's too much to expect answers to questions about pain from the one turning burning smoked on the spit. Shit. This isn't going anywhere, never mind in circles; I've joined you, you just don't know: like a ham from the rafters, I hang upside down, trussed—the tarot's Hanged One my template, the card of "sacrifice, surrender, seeing unconventionally"—I dangle by one ankle, twist in the wind, pendant on a string, bound by the cord of my desire. Ham I Am. Last supper, illumination, halo wearer, an era in which the head was called the pate. *Upon which one may play knick knack paddywhack, give the dog a bone* (a pretty dog he says, and thinks of who's walking his own), *this old man came rolling home.* What old man? He's young, and younger. And he swims like a fish in the spring of himself and he feeds on hunger. Pleasure he suspects of being his undoing. I suspect we are made to be undone, again and again, until love teaches *suffer* its name. No is the O, the concentric; how to open the O, undo the easy-for-me round of Renounce? The dead one said: For some, Lent is renunciation; for others, embrace. He didn't know how, either. O breach, preach, pleach, fruit tree, cross of the knee, crown of thorns, we are made to be (what we) desire. Its fire is to burn away the clock hands the mind hires to tick us off and away. Away, stay, O, for that country with a pond. O for twenty years gone. Gone: a fly hops his shadow from the husk of a leaf to the crust of a centipede with a mustache of brittle feet. Scan: al*right,* al*right,* our flesh is as grass; our days, the hairs of our head, numbered, pass. Numbers become numb: calculate production and deployment of paychecks, dividends of pain, debt, guilt, grief, obligation. No: to hide behind obligation. To count the cost of personal forms of nerve gas. Impasse: can not go, can not stay: the sun burns an extra moment in the day: apogee: its very shadow burns away. Invention: noon on sun dial (= faint but perceptible belief in *not fade away?*), a thing congruent with itself, a thing to long for, single.

See how the bricks make the pediment up, how the chain's shadow on it doesn't have the chain's rust. At Hiroshima, these shadows burned right in, a moment's skin become the remaining gauge of a life. The measure of my days made by the shadow of your wife.

SELF EXTENSION

The little boy in the purple shirt walks his wheelbarrow, looking. The tines of the pitch fork chatter on the orange metal, their curve like bones. He is young to be doing such work. His family is missionary. They labor together outdoors all day.

He gives me no idea, the boy. The orange is good against June green. But each word will call to certain others; certain words allow (me) to be.

A certain sensibility seated next to some universal grammar; a sensitivity to the seating chart's possibilities: the hostess with the mostest melts on her guest's tongue.

(Here, a gust(o) of breath...)

I am a guest in this country. Language bids me sit and eat. Writing is being read like sex is in the head. Wherever two or three are gathered in my name, there am I, Jesus said. The worker's tools are an extension of his body, said Marx. The pitchfork's tines do curve like ribs. And the helpmeet created where 'eye' meets 'earth'?

God is the production of syntax.

ACCORD

Sticks stick up out of the brittle leaves the leather color of winter oak. A donkey trundles its burden of cordwood and hock. Seeds arabesque a stalk, describing the shapes of Farsi to those who have eyes to hear. I'm not one, but I know what it's like. It's like here comes a shadow, the sun on my ankle, all the body's weight on my poor old ass. Jesus rode an ass into Jerusalem where the people waved palms. I wave my palm and a wind rises fast. So far I'm happy with this arrangement; I only hope it lasts.

GARY YOUNG

Gary Young is the author of five collections of poetry,
including *Days* (1997) and *Braver Deeds* (1999), both
originally published by Gibbs Smith, and reprinted in *No
Other Life* (Creative Arts Books, 2002). Among his honors
are the James D. Phelan Award, a Pushcart Prize, and
fellowships from the NEA and the California Arts Council.
He edits the *Greenhouse Review Press* and is a well-known
printer and book artist whose work is represented at the
Museum of Modern Art and The Getty Center for the Arts.
He lives in the mountains north of Santa Cruz, California.

Crushed by love, and by a war that wouldn't end, I abandoned God in nineteen sixty-eight. I thought God had abandoned us all. The world might still exist, if I could hold it in my mind, but there were people, all around me, whose lives were more desperate, and more wonderful, than anything I could imagine. There is an emptiness so great, not even the suffering of others can fill it. God is the chance that anything can happen, then it happens.

My mother was a beautiful woman. She had been a beautiful child. She danced for the soldiers, then, and sang for them, and everyone clapped and cheered. When her period came, she thought she was dying. Her face broke out, and her mother screamed, how could you do this? How will we live? Who will love you now? Years later, my mother turned to me. I was twelve. We'd stopped to rest in a little town. She put her hands on my cheeks. Let me get that, she said, and she dug her nails into me, picking until I bled. That's how it starts, she said, and it wasn't the shock or the pain, it was the look on her face that made me want to cry.

Kitty smiled, pressed my hand against the fleshy knot in her belly, and said, it's the child we always wanted, or as close as we'll ever get now. A malignancy, not a pregnancy, was swelling inside her. She'd caress it with her palms, and as the tumor grew, she mothered it; she brought it to term. One night she woke with a fever, and I carried her into the hospital. Her wasted arms and legs made her belly seem even larger than it was. A woman asked, are you in labor? And she said, no. Then the woman asked, but are you expecting? And she said, yes.

When the boy died, his father glazed a small clay jar, fired it, and filled it with the boy's ashes. Now he is in the glass house behind the garden building more pots out of clay. He works there for hours every day. He smoothes the heavy coils with his hands, and when he's finished one pot, he starts another. They're enormous.

Fishing the Powder River I found seashells at the bottom of a limestone cliff, and pulled fossils from a cutbank on Crazy Woman Creek. Even the earth has its scars and its memories. This morning a fry cook at the diner on Main Street said, there's a funeral today for that boy dropped dead in the gym. His folks will never get over this, he said. And I told him, no, they won't.

Midnight, Christmas, and a raft of stippled clouds drifts slowly across the full moon; the sky still figures in the story of our lives. This morning someone left a present at my friend's back door, and when he opened his gift the package exploded and blew away his hands. Tonight the clouds have divided the moonlight into a rainbow hung in rings around the moon: orange, red, violet, and in a thick band brighter than the rest, green, a color we seldom see in the sky at night.

My son was possessed by the Devil. Beelzebub had entered his body, and distorted his tiny features. His face was red and twisted; he gnashed his teeth, and struggled in my arms. I rapped his forehead with two fingers to drive the demon from his body, and woke up shouting, *get out, get out.* I lay in bed and listened to my wife's heavy breathing. I could hear the boy calling softly in his sleep. A hard rain fell steadily against the metal gutters, then it stopped.

When I was a young man and found I had cancer, my friends held a benefit to carry me through that difficult time. There was music and dancing, and when the night was over, they gave me a paper bag filled with cash. My wife then was always worried about money, but whenever she panicked, I reached into the sack and handed her a fistful of bills. I'll never be that rich again. Not a moment escaped me. I had everything I needed and nothing to lose. I've never been happier than when I was dying.

I was home from the hospital and not expected to survive. My mother had come to visit before I died. She needed my attention; she was still weak. She had tried to take her life again. I have trouble breathing, she said, and tapped a gold coin hanging from a choker at her throat. It's to hide the scar, she said, but the coin was too small. I gave her my hand to sit; I gave her my arm to rise. When friends arrived for dinner, she danced for an hour, beautifully. Everyone agreed she had a talent.

I am not an incidental thought of God's. Last night I had a dream. My wife and I were making love when I turned, and discovered our son had hanged himself from a beam in a corner of the room. I woke with my arms stretched out to lift the boy's limp body from the rafters; I could still feel the weight of his body in my arms. I am not an incidental thought of God's. I offer God what happens in time.

ACKNOWLEDGMENTS

NIN ANDREWS: "An Alternative to Sex," "Like an Angel," "The Message," "The Right Time," and "The Ultimate Orgasm" from *The Book of Orgasms* by Nin Andrews. Cleveland State University Poetry Center. Copyright © 2000 by Nin Andrews. Used by permission of Cleveland State University Poetry Center. "Amnesia," "Red Blossoms," "The Artichoke," "The Life of Borges," and "The Obsession" from *Why They Grow Wings* by Nin Andrews. Silverfish Review Press. Copyright © 2001 by Silverfish Review Press. Used by permission of Silverfish Review Press.

ROBERT BLY: "The Orchard Keeper" and "Warning to the Reader" from *Eating the Honey of Words: New and Selected Poems* by Robert Bly. HarperCollins. Copyright © 1999 by Robert Bly. Used by permission of HarperCollins. "A Hollow Tree," "An Octopus," "A Piece of Lichen," "Calm Day at Drake's Bay," "The Black Crab Demon," "The Crow's Head," and "Two Sounds When We Sit By the Ocean" from *What Have I Ever Lost By Dying?: Collected Prose Poems* by Robert Bly. HarperCollins. Copyright © 1992 by Robert Bly. Used by permission of HarperCollins. "An Oyster Shell" appeared in *The Best of the Prose Poem: An International Journal.* Edited by Peter Johnson. Used by permission of Robert Bly.

JOHN BRADLEY: "Crimes Against the Future" appeared in *The Prose Poem: An International Journal.* "Hawaiian Shirt" appeared in *No Exit.* "Involving the Use of the Word American" appeared in *Pacific Coast Journal.* "The History of the Clouds" appeared in *Calapooya Collage.* "Unforgiven" appeared in *Pavement Saw.* All poems Copyright © 2003 by John Bradley. Used by permission of John Bradley. "Parable of the Astral Wheel," "Parable of the Traveler from Qatar," "Parable of the White House Replica," "Three Presidents," and "To Propagate a Change in Configuration, or Bill Gates and the Blue Cow" by John Bradley. All poems Copyright © 2003. Used by permission of John Bradley.

KILLARNEY CLARY: "A small stranger without edges," "A truck pulled up," "At junctures we renamed the roads," "El Paso," "In this wind, the sharp blue cut," "No one promised to go with me," "Pieces that jammed when forced," "The boy had told a rhyme," "The man has lost his way," and "Would I dive again into" from *Potential Stranger* by Killarney Clary. The University of Chicago Press. Copyright © 2003 by Killarney Clary. Used by permission of The University of Chicago Press.

JON DAVIS: "An American," "Blues," "Brutal Squares," "In History," "Memory," "The Bait," "The Hawk. The Road. The Sunlight After Clouds," "The Sixties," "The Sorry Part," and "The Wheel of Appetite" from *Scrimmage of Appetite* by Jon Davis. The University of Akron Press. Copyright © 1995 by Jon Davis. Used by permission of The University of Akron Press.

LINDA DYER: "Farm Mutilations," "First Death in Oklahoma," "Hereditary Guess," "Level and Rise," "The Harpist, Between the Beginning and End," "The Life of the Body," "The Lost Finger," "The Seven Anxieties of Sleep," "Votive," and "Wellspring" from *Fictional Teeth* by Linda Dyer. Ahsahta Press. Copyright © 2001 by Linda Dyer. Used by permission of Ahsahta Press.

RUSSELL EDSON: "Round" and "The Glandular Condition" from *The Tormented Mirror* by Russell Edson. The University of Pittsburgh Press. Copyright © 2001 by Russell Edson. Used by permission of The University of Pittsburgh Press. "A Man Who Makes Tears," "Conjugal," "The Dark Side of the Moon," "The Family Monkey," "The Lover," "The Marionettes of Distant Masters," "The Wheel," and "Twins" from *The Tunnel: Selected Poems* by Russell Edson. Oberlin College Press. Copyright © 1994 by Russell Edson. Used by permission of Oberlin College Press.

AMY GERSTLER: "Bitter Angel," "Bzzzzz," "Difficulty at the Beginning," "Saints," "The Unforeseen," and "War Criminal" from *Bitter Angel* by Amy Gerstler. North Point Press. Copyright © 1990 by Amy Gerstler. Used by permission of Amy Gerstler. "A Lecture on Jealousy," "Slow Boat," "The Cure," and "The Holy Ghost," from *The True Bride* by Amy Gerstler. Lapis Press. Copyright © 1986 by Amy Gerstler. Used by permission of Amy Gerstler.

RAY GONZALEZ: "A Painting is Never in Love," "As If Talking," "Fucking Aztecs, Palomas, Mexico," "He Calls His Dog Rimbaud," "Joan Miro Threw a Stone at God," "The Bat," "The Black Torso of the Pharaoh," "The Blessing," "Traditional," and "Understanding" from *Human Crying Daisies* by Ray

Gonzalez. Red Hen Press. Copyright © 2003 by Ray Gonzalez. Used by permission of Red Hen Press.

MAURICE KILWEIN GUEVARA: "After Chaos Theory," "After Midnight at the Salvage Yard," "Buho, Buho," "First Apartment," "Memorial Day," "New Year's Day," "Reader of This Page," "River Spirits," and "Self-Portrait" from *Autobiography of So-and-so* by Maurice Kilwein Guevara. New Issues Press. Copyright © 2001 by Maurice Kilwein Guevara. Used by permission of New Issues Press. "The Exegesis" by Maurice Kilwein Guevara. Copyright © 2003 by Maurice Kilwein Guevara. Used by permission of Maurice Kilwein Guevara.

JUAN FELIPE HERRERA: "At the Exodus Gym/Valencia Street" and "Exiles" from *Exiles of Desire* by Juan Felipe Herrera. Arte Publico Press. Copyright © 1985 by Juan Felipe Herrera. Used by permission of Juan Felipe Herrera. "Giraffe on Fire," "Hold up the right corner of the sea, pleated," "The gold triangle is my enemy," and "Who are you?" from *Giraffe On Fire* by Juan Felipe Herrera. University of Arizona Press. Copyright © 2001 by Juan Felipe Herrera. Used by permission of The University of Arizona Press. "I, Citlalli 'La Loca' Cienfuegos: Sutra on the Notebook," "La Llorona Power-Woman Confidential," and "Taking a Bath in Aztlan" from *Notebooks of a Chile Verde Smuggler* by Juan Felipe Herrera. University of Arizona Press. Copyright © 2002 by Juan Felipe Herrera. Used by permission of The University of Arizona Press.

LOUIS JENKINS: "Laundromat," "Stone Arch, Natural Rock Formation," and "The Book" from *Just Above Water* by Louis Jenkins. Holy Cow! Press. Copyright © 1997 by Louis Jenkins. Used by permission of Holy Cow! Press. "Insects," "The Ukrainian Easter Egg," "Violence on Television," and "War Surplus" from *Nice Fish: New and Selected Prose Poems* by Louis Jenkins. Holy Cow! Press. Copyright © 1995 by Louis Jenkins. Used by permission of Holy Cow! Press. "The Bear's Money," "Somersault," and "The Name" from *The Winter Road* by Louis Jenkins. Holy Cow! Press. Copyright © 2000 by Louis Jenkins. Used by permission of Holy Cow! Press.

PETER JOHNSON: "Darwin," "Home," "Neanderthal," "Provincetown," and "Return" from *Miracles and Mortifications* by Peter Johnson. White Pine Press. Copyright © 2001 by Peter Johnson. Used by permission of White Pine Press. "Enigma of the Stigma, Or Vice Versa," "Guy Talk," "Nettles," "The Doll," and "The New Country" from *Pretty Happy!* by Peter Johnson. White Pine Press. Copyright © 1997 by Peter Johnson. Used by permission of White Pine Press.

GEORGE KALAMARAS: "A Proclitic Stitch in the Vertical Pull of Roberto Juarroz" appeared in *Untitled: A. Magazine of Prose Poetry*. "Belgisch Congo, Congo Belge" appeared in *The Louisiana Review*. "Blas de Otero and the Pantry of Blood" and "The Death of Attila Jozsef" appeared in *The Bitter Oleander*. "Lemon Seeds of Yannis Ritsos" appeared in *Luna*. "Lucien Blaga Was Not a Fish" appeared in *Turnrow*. All poems Copyright © 2003 by George Kalamaras. Used by permission of George Kalamaras. "Brahms and the Taxidermies of Sleep," "Cavafy's Craving," "To Live in Pronouns: The Birth of Pedro Salinas," and "The Sentence" Copyright © 2003 by George Kalamaras. Used by permission of George Kalamaras.

CHRISTINE BOYKA KLUGE: "Black Pearl," "Giving Away Bones," "Jar of Bees," and "The Chalk Bride" appeared in *The Bitter Oleander*. "Anatomy Woman Escapes" appeared in *Day Palm Review*. "Narcissus's Suitcase" and "Watching Her Soul From Below" appeared in *Quarter After Eight*. All poems Copyright © 2003 by Christine Boyka Kluge. Used by permission of Christine Boyka Kluge. "All of Its Words, Both Winged and Quilled," "Angel Eating Snow," and "Human With Little Sun in Her Hands" Copyright © 2003 by Christine Boyka Kluge. Used by permission of Christine Boyka Kluge.

MARY A. KONCEL: "Love Poem," "On Weeping Icons," "The Neighborhood Man," and "The Second Song of Insomnia" from *Closer to Day* by Mary A. Koncel. Quale Press. Copyright © 1999 by Mary A. Koncel. Used by permission of Mary A. Koncel. "Come Back, Elvis, Come Back to Holyoke," appeared in *The Illinois Review*. "The Lake Shore Limited" appeared in *The Denver Quarterly*. "The Year of the Man" appeared in *The Party Train: A Collection of North American Prose Poetry*. New Rivers Press. All poems Copyright © 2003 by Mary A. Koncel. "Bump," "Meditation on a Bird Sitting on a Man's Head," and "When the Babies Are Missing Again," Copyright © 2003 by Mary A. Koncel. Used by permission of Mary A. Koncel.

MORTON MARCUS: "Goodbye to the Twentieth Century," "Moon and Flower," and "The Face" from *Moments Without Names: New and Selected Prose Poems* by Morton Marcus. White Pine Press.